Pattern Explorer

Level 1

Pattern Explorer products available in print or eBook form.

Beginning • Level 1 • Level 2

Written by
Darin Beigie

Graphic Design by
Scott Slyter

© 2014
THE CRITICAL THINKING CO.™
www.CriticalThinking.com
Phone: 800-458-4849 • Fax: 541-756-1758
1991 Sherman Ave., Suite 200 • North Bend • OR 97459
ISBN 978-1-60144-713-5

 MIX
Paper from
responsible sources
FSC® C011935

Table of Contents

About the Author

Darin Beigie teaches mathematics at Harvard-Westlake School in Los Angeles, CA. He develops curriculum and classroom materials to foster greater critical thinking and creativity amongst his students. He publishes frequently in education and teaching journals. He is the author of other books by The Critical Thinking Co.™, including the award-winning *Mathematical Reasoning™ Middle School Supplement* (Grades 7-9), *Math Analogies Level 3* (Grades 6-7), *Math Analogies Level 4* (Grades 8-9) and *Pattern Explorer Level 2* (Grades 7-9). Darin began his career with a Ph.D. in Theoretical Physics at the California Institute of Technology in Pasadena, CA, followed by a Research and Teaching Fellowship at Cornell University's Center for Applied Mathematics in Ithaca, NY. Darin's volunteer work at public middle schools inspired him to become a school teacher, and he has since taught middle school mathematics in New York, Massachusetts, and California.

Introduction

Mathematics and science can be thought of as a search for patterns and structure. Discovery and insight comes when patterns are recognized and structure is understood. From a developmental perspective, the ability to recognize a pattern signals the transition from concrete to abstract thinking. So having children explore pattern problems helps sensitize them to the discovery process that provides a foundation for authentic learning and abstraction.

The pattern problems in this collection are divided into five themes: Pattern Predictor, Equality Explorer, Sequence Sleuth, Number Ninja, and Function Finder. To maximize diversity and variation, these themes appear in rotating order for a total of 40 activity sets (eight sets per theme). The activities are independent and self-contained, but they tend to build on one another and get slightly more sophisticated as the collection progresses. So students are generally encouraged to work on the earlier sets first and build up from there, although they should feel free to pick and choose as well.

The patterns are appropriate for students in Grades 5-7, although their experiences with these activities may vary widely depending upon readiness for abstraction. Younger students may find each activity to be like a small project, worthy of rich exploration and deep thinking. Older students may be equipped to uncover patterns with much greater agility and speed. In all situations, and at whatever pace and facility, the transition from concrete to abstract thinking is worthwhile.

All activities provide space for work to be shown, but students are encouraged to have scratch paper at hand in case uncovering a pattern merits deeper investigation, such as guess-and-check, drawing diagrams, and making lists or charts. Calculators are never needed, and their use is discouraged. Occasionally, more difficult arithmetic might tempt a student to reach for a calculator. Since the emphasis is on pattern recognition and not arithmetic, we leave it to teacher discretion about whether occasional calculator use will be permitted. This collection deliberately avoids use of variables, but the activities involve reasoning that lays a genuine foundation for algebraic thinking and technique.

Each activity is accompanied by hints and solutions, in separate sections following the activities. The hints provide occasional nudges to help steer a student in the right direction. The solutions are generally detailed and comprehensive. There are many ways to solve and explain a pattern problem, and the solutions provided are not intended to be unique. The student may come up with many other wonderful ways to solve and describe the patterns. The answers, however, are usually unique.

The teacher should encourage students to pursue these pattern problems with a sense of adventure and perseverance. Some pattern discoveries may come quickly, while others may require patience and determination. Regardless, the pattern exploration offers rich and authentic experiences in mathematical reasoning.

1. Pattern Predictor 1

Look at the pattern of circles to answer the questions below.

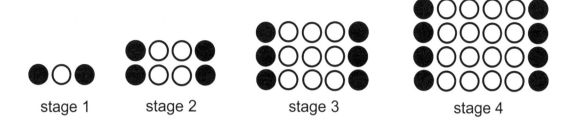

stage 1   stage 2   stage 3   stage 4

1. How many unshaded circles ○ are there at stage 9?

2. How many shaded circles ● are there at stage 12?

3. What is the total number of circles at stage 15?

4. At what stage are there 14 shaded circles?

5. At what stage are there 400 unshaded circles?

1. Pattern Predictor 1 (continued)

Look at the pattern of diamonds to answer the questions below.

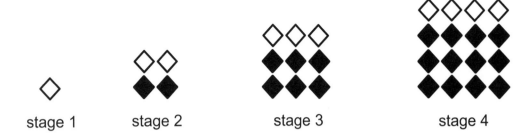

stage 1   stage 2   stage 3   stage 4

6. How many unshaded diamonds ◇ are there at stage 10?

7. How many shaded diamonds ◆ are there at stage 7?

8. What is the total number of diamonds at stage 12?

9. At what stage are there 45 unshaded diamonds?

10. At what stage is there a total of 100 diamonds?

2. Equality Explorer 1

Each 2D shape represents a different whole number. Use the balance scales to find their value.

1.

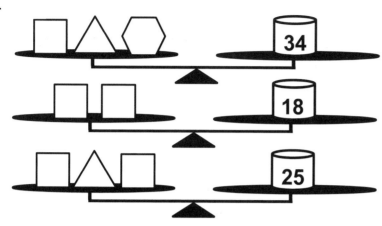

2.

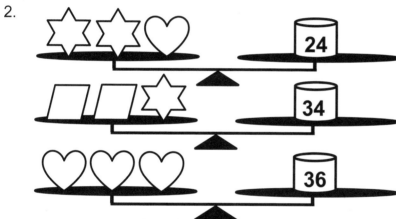

3.

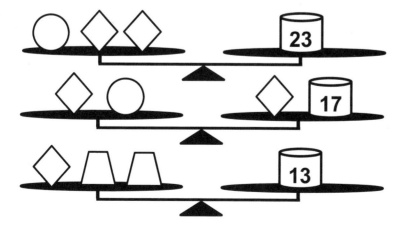

3. Sequence Sleuth 1

Look at the shading pattern to answer the questions below.

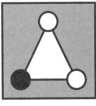 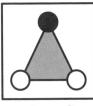
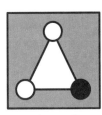
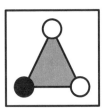
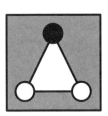

| stage 1 | stage 2 | stage 3 | stage 4 | stage 5 |

1. Draw the shading pattern for each of the stages.

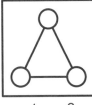 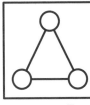
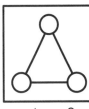
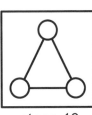
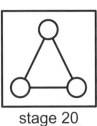

| stage 6 | stage 7 | stage 8 | stage 13 | stage 20 |

note stage numbers

2. What is the next stage number after stage 20 that has shading identical to stage 20?

3. List all stage numbers less than 25 that have gray shading inside the triangle.

4. List all stage numbers less than 25 that have the top circle filled in.

5. List all stage numbers less than 25 that have gray shading inside the triangle and the top circle filled in.

6. List all stage numbers less than 50 that have shading identical to stage 1.

4. Number Ninja 1

1. Fill in each empty circle with a fraction so that each side of the square adds up to 1.

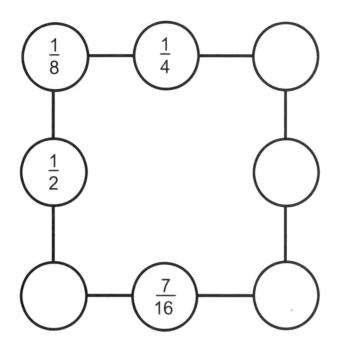

2. Use the numbers 1, 2, 3, 4, 5, 6 to fill in the circles to make the equations true. Use each number exactly once.

◯ + ◯ x ◯ = 21

◯ x ◯ ÷ ◯ = 9

3. Use the numbers 4, 5, 6, 7, 8, 9 to fill in the circles to make the equations true. Use each number exactly once.

◯ x ◯ – ◯ = 49

◯ – ◯ ÷ ◯ = 5

5. Function Finder 1

The function machine multiplies by 7. So when you input 9, the output is 63.

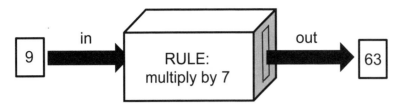

1. If you input 12, what is the output?   2. If the output is 140, what is the input?

3. Each question shows a table for a different function machine. State the rule for the function machine and fill in the missing numbers.

a.

in	out
3	12
5	20
8	32
12	48
15	60
21	84
25	100
40	
	208

RULE:

b.

in	out
1	7
4	10
6	12
9	15
14	20
18	24
25	31
38	
	63

RULE:

c.

in	out
27	3
45	5
72	8
90	10
99	11
135	15
180	20
225	
	37

RULE:

d.

in	out
10	2
14	6
18	10
20	12
25	17
50	42
74	66
88	
	92

RULE:

6. Pattern Predictor 2

The figures below are constructed from shaded triangles. Stage 1 has 3 shaded triangles. Stage 2 has 10 shaded triangles.

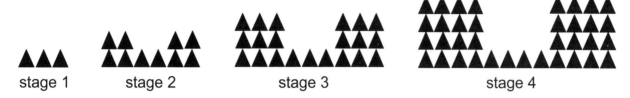

stage 1   stage 2   stage 3   stage 4

1. How many shaded triangles are there at stage 3?

2. How many shaded triangles are there at stage 4?

3. How many shaded triangles are there at stage 6?

4. How many shaded triangles are there at stage 9?

5. At what stage are there exactly 136 shaded triangles?

6. How many shaded triangles are there at stage 15?

7. At what stage are there exactly 300 shaded triangles?

6. Pattern Predictor 2 (continued)

Look at the pattern of hearts to answer the questions below.

stage 1   stage 2   stage 3   stage 4

8. How many hearts are there at stage 5?

9. How many hearts are there at stage 8?

10. How many hearts are there at stage 11?

11. At what stage are there 104 hearts?

12. How many hearts are there at stage 19?

13. At what stage are there 68 hearts?

7. Equality Explorer 2

Each 2D shape represents a different whole number. Use the balance scales to answer the questions.

1.

What is the value of 🌥️? Explain.

2.

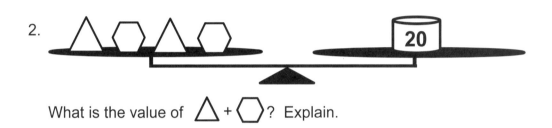

What is the value of △ + ⬡? Explain.

3.

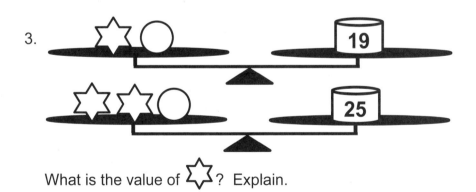

What is the value of ✡? Explain.

8. Sequence Sleuth 2

Look at the pattern of shapes to answer the questions below.

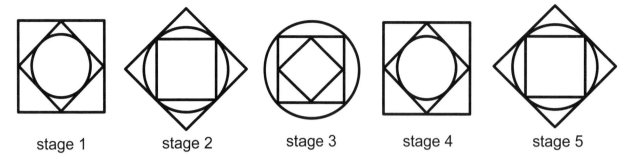

stage 1   stage 2   stage 3   stage 4   stage 5

1. Draw the shape for each of the stages.

stage 6   stage 7   stage 14   stage 19

note stage numbers

2. List all stage numbers less than 25 that have the same shape as in stage 2.

3. List all stage numbers between 20 and 30 that have the same shape as in stage 1.

4. Draw the shape in stage 40.

5. Draw the shape in stage 50.

9. Number Ninja 2

Fill in each empty circle with a number so that the sum of the numbers in any two circles equals the number between them.

1.
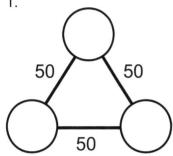

2.
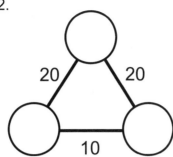

3.
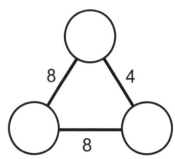

4.
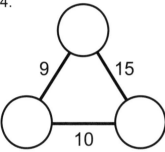

5.
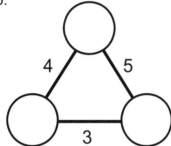

6.
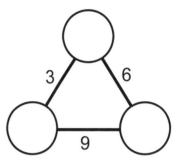

7.
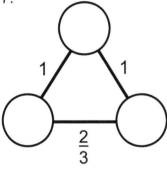

8.
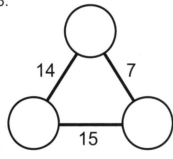

9.
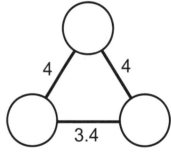

10.
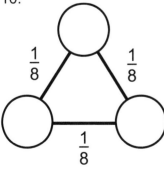

11.
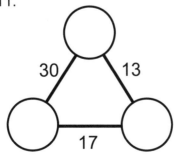

12.
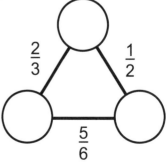

10. Function Finder 2

The function machine multiplies by 2 and then adds 3. So when you input 6, the output is 15.

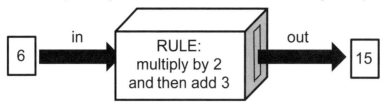

1. If you input 11, what is the output?   2. If the output is 13, what is the input?

3. Each question shows a table for a different function machine. State the rule for the function machine and fill in the missing numbers.

a.

in	out
0	1
3	7
6	13
10	21
13	27
20	41
25	51
34	
	127

RULE:

b.

in	out
0	2
2	12
3	17
6	32
8	42
20	102
25	127
32	
	202

RULE:

c.

in	out
0	3
1	10
2	17
3	24
4	31
6	45
10	73
25	
	213

RULE:

d.

in	out
0	10
1	16
2	22
3	28
5	40
8	58
15	100
20	
	310

RULE:

11. Pattern Predictor 3

stage 1   stage 2   stage 3   stage 4

1. How many stars are there
    at stage 5?

2. How many stars are there
    at stage 8?

3. How many stars are there
    at stage 15?

4. At what stage are there 50 stars?

5. How many stars are there
    at stage 20?

6. At what stage are there 42 stars?

11. Pattern Predictor 3 (continued)

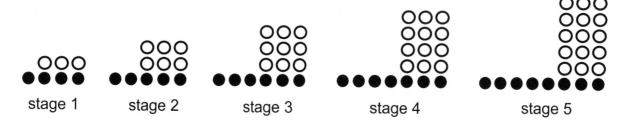

stage 1   stage 2   stage 3   stage 4   stage 5

7. How many unshaded circles are there at stage 12?

8. How many shaded circles are there at stage 17?

9. What is the total number of circles at stage 10?

10. At what stage are there 24 unshaded circles?

11. At what stage are there 25 shaded circles?

12. What is the total number of circles at stage 20?

12. Equality Explorer 3

Each 2D shape represents a different whole number. Use the balance scales to answer the questions.

1.

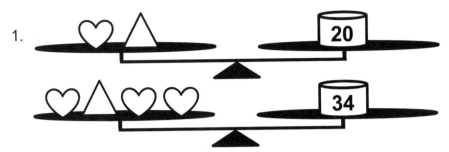

What is the value of ♡? Explain.

2.

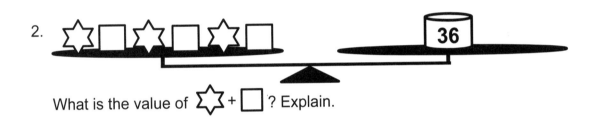

What is the value of ☆ + ▢ ? Explain.

3.

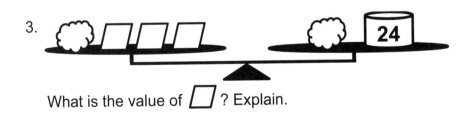

What is the value of ▱ ? Explain.

13. Sequence Sleuth 3

Look at the clock pattern to answer the questions below.

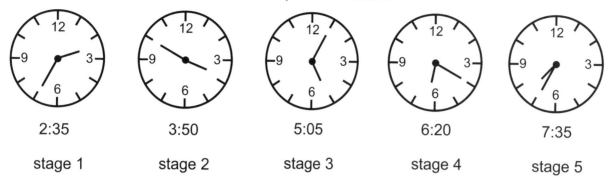

2:35	3:50	5:05	6:20	7:35
stage 1	stage 2	stage 3	stage 4	stage 5

1. For each stage, draw the clock hands and write the time below the clock.

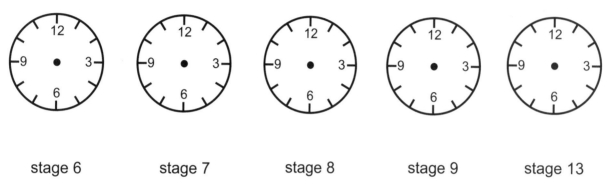

stage 6   stage 7   stage 8   stage 9   stage 13

2. List the times for stages 1, 5, 9, and 13. What pattern do you see?

3. Use the pattern in question 2 to help you determine the answers to the following questions.

   a. What is the time at stage 17?   b. What is the time at stage 29?

4. List the times for stages 2, 6, 10, 14.   5. What is the time at stage 22?

14. Number Ninja 3

1. For the sequence of operations below, if you start with 10 you end with 38.

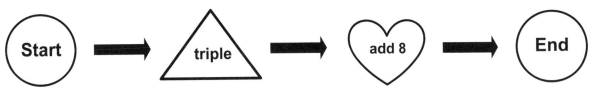

   a. If you start with 16, you end with what number?

   b. If you end with 14, you start with what number?

2. For the sequence of operations below, if you start with 41 you end with 15.

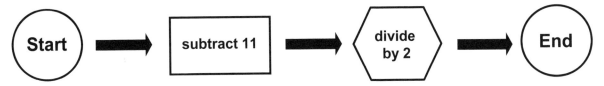

   a. If you start with 77, you end with what number?

   b. If you end with 5, you start with what number?

3. For the sequence of operations below, if you start with 30 you end with 24.

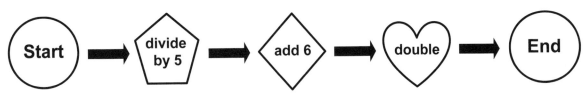

   a. If you start with 70, you end with what number?

   b. If you end with 32, you start with what number?

15. Function Finder 3

Each question gives examples of a secret operation acting upon two numbers. Look for a pattern to understand how the operation works. Then fill in the blanks.

1.

Examples:	6 ♥ 7 = 43	9 ♥ 10 = 91	7 ♥ 4 = 29
	8 ♥ 3 = 25	2 ♥ 5 = 11	3 ♥ 10 = 31

a. 5 ♥ 9 = ____

b. 16 ♥ 3 = ____

c. 4 ♥ 8 = ____

d. ____ ♥ 20 = 101

e. 6 ♥ ____ = 19

f. ____ ♥ 11 = 78

2.

Examples:	10 ♦ 20 = 15	13 ♦ 1 = 7	25 ♦ 75 = 50
	14 ♦ 6 = 10	12 ♦ 14 = 13	5 ♦ 9 = 7

a. 8 ♦ 12 = ____

b. 3 ♦ 21 = ____

c. 17 ♦ 33 = ____

d. ____ ♦ 8 = 5

e. 15 ♦ ____ = 10

f. ____ ♦ 30 = 27

3.

Examples:	3 ♣ 2 = 10	2 ♣ 7 = 18	10 ♣ 1 = 22
	0 ♣ 8 = 16	13 ♣ 2 = 30	5 ♣ 4 = 18

a. 3 ♣ 7 = ____

b. 9 ♣ 5 = ____

c. 10 ♣ 6 = ____

d. ____ ♣ 4 = 12

e. 8 ♣ ____ = 30

f. ____ ♣ 10 = 26

16. Pattern Predictor 4

The pattern consists of shaded ● and unshaded ○ circles.

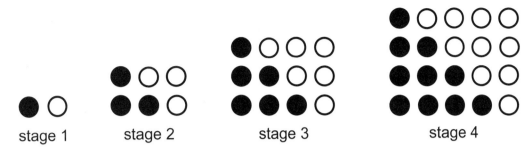

stage 1   stage 2   stage 3   stage 4

1. What is the total number of circles
    in stage 5?

2. How many unshaded circles are
    there in stage 5?

3. What is the total number of circles
    in stage 6?

4. How many shaded circles are there
    in stage 6?

5. What is the total number of circles
    in stage 10?

6. How many unshaded circles are there
    in stage 10?

16. Pattern Predictor 4 (continued)

7. At what stage will there be a total of 72 circles? How many of these circles are unshaded?

8. At what stage will there be 45 shaded circles? What is the total number of circles at this stage?

9. How many shaded circles will there be at stage 11?

10. How many unshaded circles will there be at stage 12?

11. How many circles will there be at stage 20?

12. At what stage number will there be 28 shaded circles?

17. Equality Explorer 4

Each 2D shape represents a different whole number. Use the balance scales to find their value.

1.

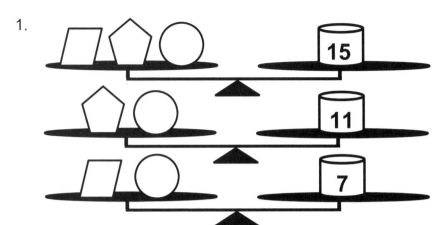

2.

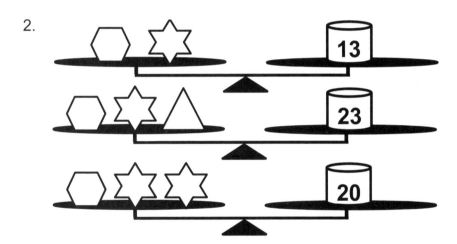

3.

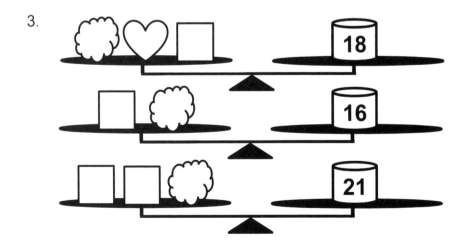

18. Sequence Sleuth 4

Look at the pattern to answer the questions below.

1 1 1 1 2 2 2 2 3

term 1   term 2   term 3   term 4   term 5   term 6   term 7   term 8   term 9

1. Draw each of the terms.

term 13   term 14   term 15   term 16   term 17   term 18   term 19   term 20

2. Draw each of the terms.

   a. term 10   b. term 11   c. term 22

   d. term 25   e. term 27   f. term 30

   g. term 31   h. term 33   i. term 36

19. Number Ninja 4

1. Use the numbers $\frac{1}{3}$, $\frac{2}{3}$, $\frac{5}{6}$, $1\frac{1}{6}$, $1\frac{1}{2}$ to fill in the empty circles so that each side of the square adds up to 2. Use each number exactly once.

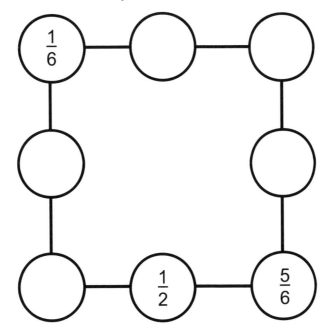

2. Place an operation sign (+, −, x, or ÷) in each blank space to make the equation true. The first one is done as an example.

   a. 2 __+__ 3 __x__ 6 = 20

   b. 12 ___ 2 ___ 3 = 6

   c. 20 ___ 3 ___ 10 = 13

   d. 4 ___ 8 ___ 3 ___ 9 = 5

   e. 6 ___ 6 ___ 3 ___ 9 = 3

   f. 16 ___ 18 ___ 6 ___ 11 = 30

20. Function Finder 4

The function machine divides by 3 and then adds 5. So when you input 36, the output is 17.

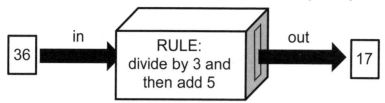

1. If you input 54, what is the output?   2. If the output is 11, what is the input?

3. Each question shows a table for a different function machine. State the rule for the function machine and fill in the missing numbers.

a.

in	out
24	3
40	5
72	9
88	11
120	15
200	25
240	30
320	
	60

RULE:

b.

in	out
20	11
40	21
100	51
200	101
500	251
800	401
900	451
1,000	
	1,201

RULE:

c.

in	out
0	100
4	102
6	103
14	107
30	115
66	133
88	144
160	
	500

RULE:

d.

in	out
24	2
36	3
60	5
72	6
120	10
180	15
240	20
360	
	45

RULE:

21. Pattern Predictor 5

The figures below are constructed from unit squares. Stage 2 has 4 unit squares:
3 shaded and 1 unshaded.

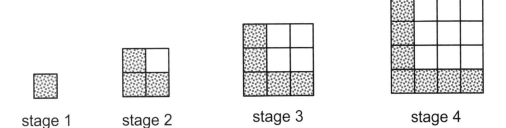

| stage 1 | stage 2 | stage 3 | stage 4 |

1. Complete the table to describe the pattern.

stage	1	2	3	4	5	6	7	8
# of unshaded unit squares	0	1						
# of shaded unit squares	1	3						
total # of unit squares	1	4						

2. How many unshaded unit squares are there at stage 11?

3. How many shaded unit squares are there at stage 14?

4. What is the total number of unit squares at stage 15?

5. At what stage are there 35 shaded unit squares?

21. Pattern Predictor 5 (continued)

The figures below are constructed from unit squares. Stage 1 has 9 unit squares:
8 shaded and 1 unshaded.

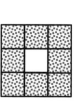

stage 1

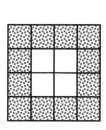

stage 2

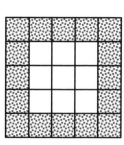

stage 3

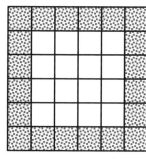

stage 4

6. Complete the table to describe the pattern.

stage	1	2	3	4	5	6	7	8
# of unshaded unit squares	1							
# of shaded unit squares	8							
total # of unit squares	9							

7. How many unshaded unit squares are there at stage 12?

8. How many shaded unit squares are there at stage 11?

9. What is the total number of unit squares at stage 13?

10. At what stage are there 72 shaded unit squares?

22. Equality Explorer 5

Each 2D shape represents a different whole number. Use the balance scales to find their value.

1.

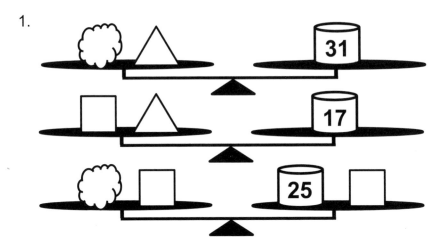

2.

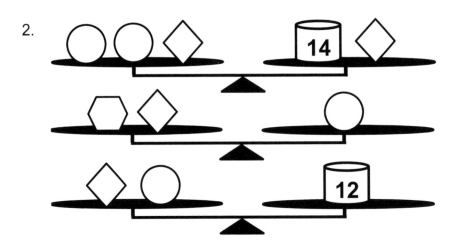

3.

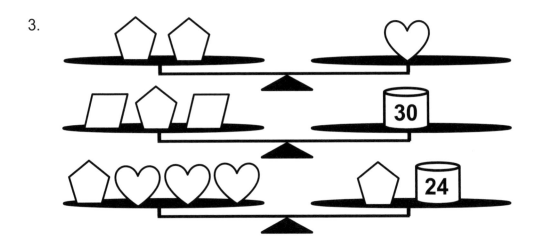

23. Sequence Sleuth 5

Look at the pattern to answer the questions below.

stage 1   stage 2   stage 3   stage 4   stage 5   stage 6   stage 7

1. Draw the figure for each of the stages.

    stage 8   stage 9   stage 10   stage 11   stage 12   stage 13   stage 14

2. Draw stage 17.   3. Draw stage 21.   4. Draw stage 24.

5. What is the next stage number after stage 2 that has a figure identical to stage 2?

6. What is the next stage number after stage 5 that has a figure identical to stage 5?

7. List all stage numbers less than 50 that have the arrow pointing up.

8. List all stage numbers less than 50 that have exactly 1 shaded circle.

9. List all stage numbers less than 50 that have the arrow pointing up and exactly 1 shaded circle.

10. List all stage numbers less than 50 that have the arrow pointing up and exactly 2 shaded circles.

24. Number Ninja 5

1. Fill in each empty square with a number so that each row, each column, and each diagonal add up to $\frac{1}{2}$.

	$\frac{3}{10}$	
	$\frac{1}{6}$	
$\frac{4}{15}$		

2. Place an operation sign (+, −, x, or ÷) in each blank space to make the equation true.

a. 4 ___ 4 ___ 4 ___ 4 = 0

b. 4 ___ 4 ___ 4 ___ 4 = 2

c. 4 ___ 4 ___ 4 ___ 4 = 7

d. 4 ___ 4 ___ 4 ___ 4 = 8

e. 4 ___ 4 ___ 4 ___ 4 = 9

f. 4 ___ 4 ___ 4 ___ 4 = 16

g. 4 ___ 4 ___ 4 ___ 4 = 17

h. 4 ___ 4 ___ 4 ___ 4 = 24

i. 4 ___ 4 ___ 4 ___ 4 = 32

j. 4 ___ 4 ___ 4 ___ 4 = 60

25. Function Finder 5

Each question gives examples of a secret operation acting upon two numbers. Look for a pattern to understand how the operation works. Then fill in the blanks.

1.

Examples:	4 ♠ 10 = 20	8 ♠ 6 = 24	3 ♠ 22 = 33
	6 ♠ 7 = 21	3 ♠ 4 = 6	5 ♠ 10 = 25

a. 8 ♠ 9 = _____

b. 4 ♠ 14 = _____

c. 16 ♠ 2 = _____

d. _____ ♠ 20 = 50

e. 3 ♠ _____ = 27

f. _____ ♠ 11 = 44

2.

Examples:	40 Ω 20 = 59	25 Ω 10 = 34	12 Ω 8 = 19
	14 Ω 14 = 27	13 Ω 18 = 30	9 Ω 4 = 12

a. 11 Ω 15 = _____

b. 17 Ω 30 = _____

c. 6 Ω 12 = _____

d. _____ Ω 13 = 18

e. 7 Ω _____ = 25

f. _____ Ω 95 = 129

3.

Examples:	9 ↔ 3 = 270	5 ↔ 9 = 450	8 ↔ 1 = 80
	6 ↔ 6 = 360	14 ↔ 5 = 700	11 ↔ 4 = 440

a. 8 ↔ 5 = _____

b. 6 ↔ 4 = _____

c. 2 ↔ 19 = _____

d. _____ ↔ 7 = 280

e. 3 ↔ _____ = 540

f. _____ ↔ 10 = 1,000

26. Pattern Predictor 6

A banquet has pentagonal tables, joined together as shown. There is one seat for each exposed table edge.

Here is a banquet with only 1 table.

Here is a banquet with 2 tables.

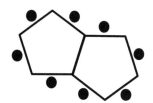

Here is a banquet with 3 tables.

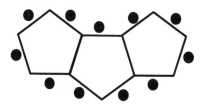

1. Complete the table to describe the pattern.

# of tables	1	2	3	4	5	6	7	8
# of seats								

2. How many seats are there if the banquet has 12 tables?

3. If the banquet has 50 seats, how many tables are there?

4. How many seats are there if the banquet has 30 tables?

5. If the banquet has 71 seats, how many tables are there?

26. Pattern Predictor 6 (continued)

A banquet has octagonal tables, joined together as shown. There is one seat for each exposed table edge.

Here is a banquet with only 1 table.

Here is a banquet with 2 tables.

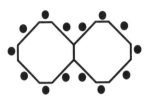

Here is a banquet with 3 tables.

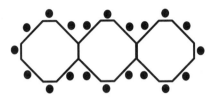

6. Complete the table to describe the pattern.

# of tables	1	2	3	4	5	6	7	8
# of seats								

7. How many seats are there if the banquet has 13 tables?

8. If the banquet has 62 seats, how many tables are there?

9. How many seats are there if the banquet has 33 tables?

10. If the banquet has 152 seats, how many tables are there?

27. Equality Explorer 6

Each 2D shape represents a different whole number. Use the balance scales to find their value.

1.

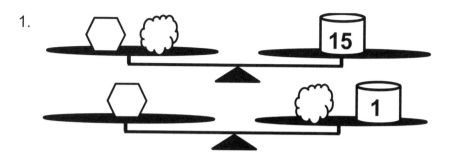

2.

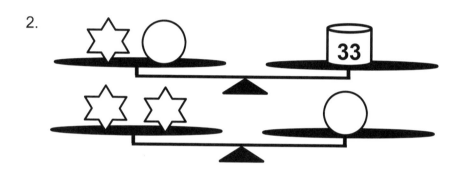

3.

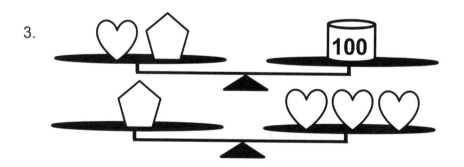

4.

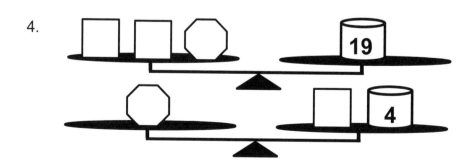

28. Sequence Sleuth 6

For each sequence, find the pattern to answer the questions.

1. L, M, N, O, P, L, M, N, O, P, L, …

    1st term

    a. 20th term = _____
    b. 28th term = _____
    c. 51st term = _____

    d. 87th term = _____
    e. 99th term = _____
    f. 782nd term = _____

2. a, b, c, a, b, c, a, b, c, a, …

    a. 18th term = _____
    b. 32nd term = _____
    c. 67th term = _____

    d. 92nd term = _____
    e. 100th term = _____
    f. 300th term = _____

3. a, b, b, c, c, c, d, d, d, d, e, e, e, e, e, f, …

    a. 20th term = _____
    b. 22nd term = _____
    c. 30th term = _____

    d. 40th term = _____
    e. 55th term = _____
    f. 56th term = _____

4. f, G, h, F, g, H, f, G, h, F, g, H, f, …

    a. 24th term = _____
    b. 26th term = _____
    c. 60th term = _____

    d. 64th term = _____
    e. 121st term = _____
    f. 125th term = _____

5. A1, B2, C3, A4, B1, C2, A3, B4, C1, A2, B3, C4, A1, B2, …

    a. 15th term = _____
    b. 18th term = _____
    c. 22nd term = _____

    d. 24th term = _____
    e. 36th term = _____
    f. 38th term = _____

29. Number Ninja 6

1. For the sequence of operations below, if you start with 9 you end with 20.

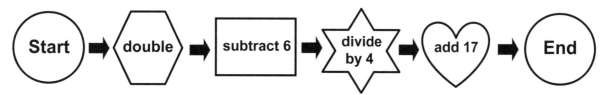

   a. If you start with 19, you end with what number?

   b. If you end with 42, you start with what number?

2. For the sequence of operations below, if you start with 40 you end with 193.

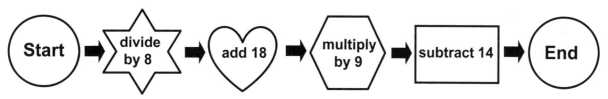

   a. If you start with 64, you end with what number?

   b. If you end with 166, you start with what number?

3. For the sequence of operations below, if you start with 3 you end with 6.

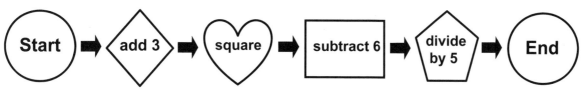

   a. If you start with 6, you end with what number?

   b. If you end with 2, you start with what number?

30. Function Finder 6

Each question shows a table for a different function machine. State the rule for the function machine and fill in the missing numbers.

1.

in	out
15	6
22	13
30	21
39	30
47	38
51	42
76	67
167	
	193

RULE:

2.

in	out
0	0
2	22
3	33
5	55
8	88
10	110
12	132
15	
	275

RULE:

3.

in	out
0	3
1	13
4	43
6	63
9	93
12	123
20	203
27	
	413

RULE:

4.

in	out
12	2
18	3
30	5
48	8
66	11
120	20
150	25
270	
	150

RULE:

5.

in	out
3	9
4	16
5	25
7	49
8	64
10	100
12	144
15	
	400

RULE:

6.

in	out
2	17
6	21
11	26
20	35
29	44
38	53
52	67
73	
	177

RULE:

31. Pattern Predictor 7

Unit cubes 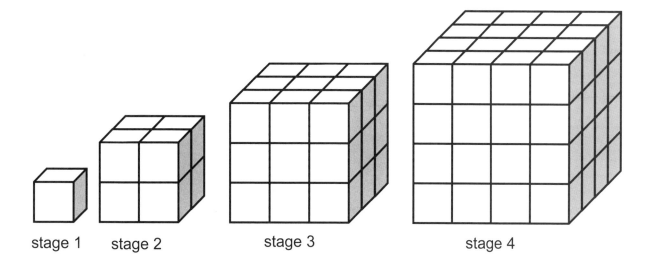 are joined together to build larger cubes. For example:

- The stage 2 cube is built from 8 unit cubes: 4 on top and 4 on the bottom.

- The stage 2 cube's surface contains 24 unit squares: 4 on top, 4 on the bottom, 4 in the front, 4 in the back, 4 on the right, and 4 on the left.

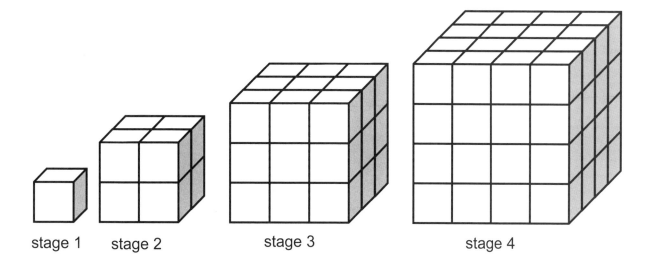

stage 1   stage 2   stage 3   stage 4

1. How many unit cubes are there at stage 3?

2. How many unit cubes are there at stage 4?

3. The stage 3 cube's surface contains how many unit squares?

4. The stage 4 cube's surface contains how many unit squares?

31. Pattern Predictor 7 (continued)

5. Complete the table to describe the pattern.

stage	1	2	3	4	5	6	7
# of unit cubes	1	8					
# of unit squares on the cube's surface	6	24					

6. How many unit cubes are there at stage 10?

7. The stage 10 cube's surface contains how many unit squares?

8. What is the smallest stage number for which there are at least 500 unit cubes?

9. The stage 4 cube is cut into two halves, and the bottom half is shown.

   a. The resulting shape contains how many unit cubes?

   b. The resulting shape's surface contains how many unit squares?

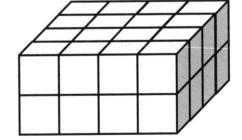

32. Equality Explorer 7

Each 2D shape represents a different whole number. Use the balance scales to find their value.

1.

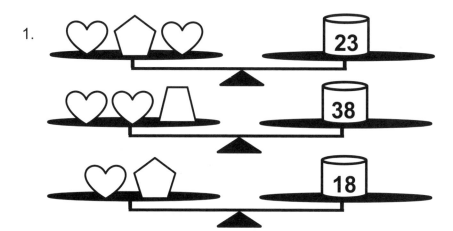

2.

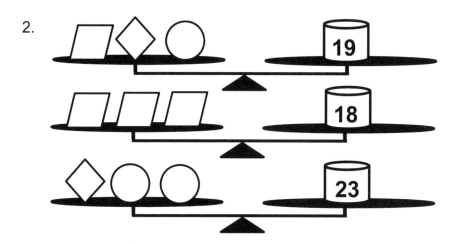

3.

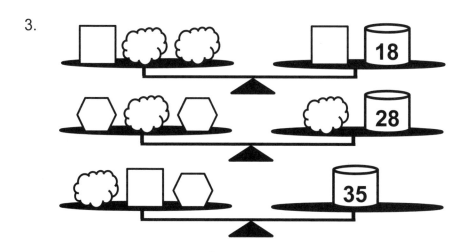

33. Sequence Sleuth 7

Look at the pattern to answer the questions below.

A ∀ ∀ ◁ B ᗺ B ꓭ C

term 1   term 2   term 3   term 4   term 5   term 6   term 7   term 8   term 9

1. Draw each of the terms.

term 10   term 11   term 12   term 17   term 18   term 19   term 20   term 23

2. Draw each of the terms.

   a. term 25   b. term 28   c. term 30   d. term 37

   e. term 39   f. term 42   g. term 44   h. term 49

   i. term 50   j. term 52   k. term 61   l. term 63

34. Number Ninja 7

Each question gives 5 examples of a diamond filled with 4 numbers related by a secret pattern. Discover the pattern and then fill in the missing numbers.

1.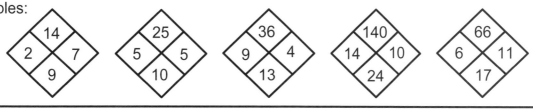

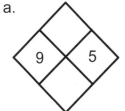 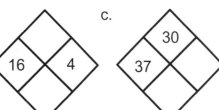 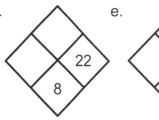 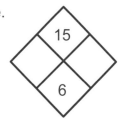

2.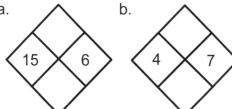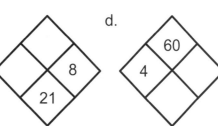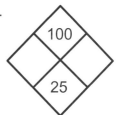

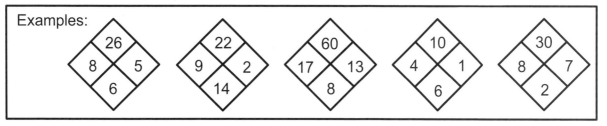

3.

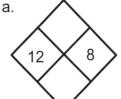  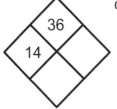 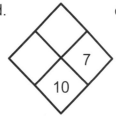 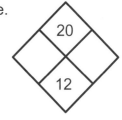

35. Function Finder 7

Each question gives examples of a secret operation acting upon two numbers. Look for a pattern to understand how the operation works. Then fill in the blanks.

1.
Examples:	$13 \,☼\, 27 = \dfrac{1}{40}$	$75 \,☼\, 25 = \dfrac{1}{100}$	$32 \,☼\, 43 = \dfrac{1}{75}$
	$17 \,☼\, 12 = \dfrac{1}{29}$	$3 \,☼\, 5 = \dfrac{1}{8}$	$11 \,☼\, 11 = \dfrac{1}{22}$

a. $4 \,☼\, 8 =$ _____

b. $9 \,☼\, 44 =$ _____

c. $21 \,☼\, 39 =$ _____

d. _____ $☼\, 9 = \dfrac{1}{37}$

e. $15 \,☼\,$ _____ $= \dfrac{1}{88}$

f. _____ $☼\, 24 = \dfrac{1}{48}$

2.
Examples:	$87 \,♫\, 34 = 530$	$20 \,♫\, 7 = 130$	$100 \,♫\, 21 = 790$
	$15 \,♫\, 4 = 110$	$54 \,♫\, 30 = 240$	$22 \,♫\, 19 = 30$

a. $18 \,♫\, 13 =$ _____

b. $28 \,♫\, 18 =$ _____

c. $32 \,♫\, 1 =$ _____

d. _____ $♫\, 9 = 310$

e. $15 \,♫\,$ _____ $= 10$

f. _____ $♫\, 40 = 450$

3.
Examples:	$10 \,◄\, 3 = 23$	$50 \,◄\, 9 = 109$	$15 \,◄\, 7 = 37$
	$75 \,◄\, 8 = 158$	$100 \,◄\, 6 = 206$	$5 \,◄\, 1 = 11$

a. $18 \,◄\, 6 =$ _____

b. $20 \,◄\, 5 =$ _____

c. $7 \,◄\, 3 =$ _____

d. _____ $◄\, 4 = 26$

e. $44 \,◄\,$ _____ $= 101$

f. _____ $◄\, 10 = 80$

36. Pattern Predictor 8

The figures below are constructed from unit triangles. Stage 2 has 4 unit triangles: 3 shaded and 1 unshaded.

stage 1   stage 2   stage 3   stage 4

1. Complete the table to describe the pattern.

stage	1	2	3	4	5	6	7	8
# of unshaded unit triangles	0	1						
# of shaded unit triangles	1	3						
total # of unit triangles	1	4						

2. How many shaded unit triangles are there at stage 12?

3. How many unshaded unit triangles are there at stage 11?

4. What is the total number of unit triangles at stage 14?

5. At what stage is there a total of 900 unit triangles?

36. Pattern Predictor 8 (continued)

The figures below are constructed from unit squares.

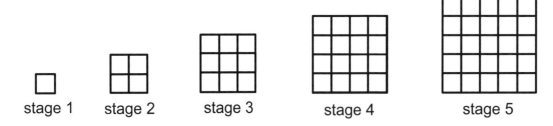

stage 1   stage 2   stage 3   stage 4   stage 5

For this activity, we count the number of squares of any size. For example, stage 2 contains 5 squares:

6. How many squares of any size are there at stage 3?

7. How many squares of any size are there at stage 4?

8. How many squares of any size are there at stage 5?

9. How many squares of any size are there at stage 6?

10. How many squares of any size are there at stage 7?

11. How many squares of any size are there at stage 8?

37. Equality Explorer 8

Each 2D shape represents a different whole number. Use the balance scales to find their value.

1.

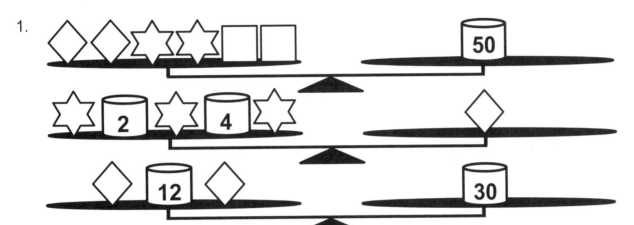

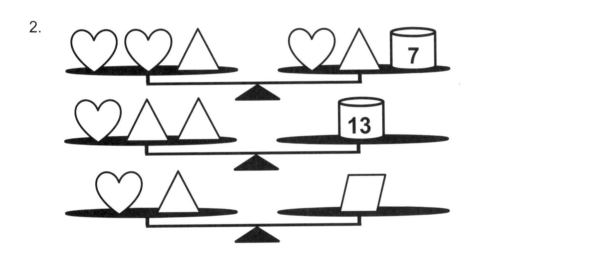

2.

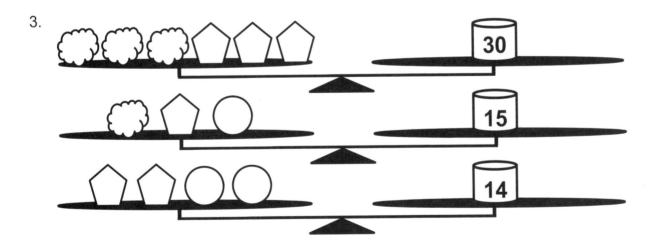

3.

38. Sequence Sleuth 8

Give the next three numbers in the sequence and then the indicated number. Give fractions in simplified form.

1. 8, 13, 18, 23, 28, _____, _____, _____
$\uparrow$
1st number

20th number = _____

2. 4, 7, 10, 13, 16, _____, _____, _____

25th number = _____

3. 900, 885, 870, 855, 840, _____, _____, _____

15th number = _____

4. $1\frac{3}{4}$, $2\frac{3}{8}$, 3, $3\frac{5}{8}$, $4\frac{1}{4}$, _____, _____, _____

10th number = _____

5. 50, $47\frac{2}{3}$, $45\frac{1}{3}$, 43, $40\frac{2}{3}$, _____, _____, _____

10th number = _____

6. 1, 3, 6, 10, 15, 21, 28, _____, _____, _____

15th number = _____

7. 4, 2, 1, $\frac{1}{2}$, $\frac{1}{4}$, $\frac{1}{8}$, _____, _____, _____

12th number = _____

8. 2, 6, 12, 20, 30, 42, 56, _____, _____, _____

15th number = _____

39. Number Ninja 8

Each question gives 5 examples of a center number related to 3 circled numbers by a secret pattern. Discover the pattern and then fill in the missing numbers.

1. Examples:

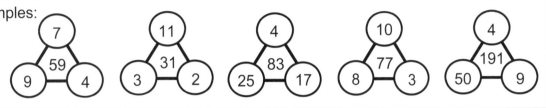

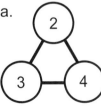 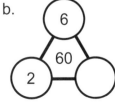 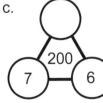 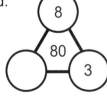 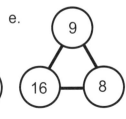

2. Examples:

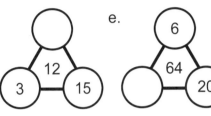

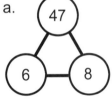 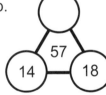 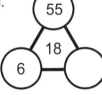 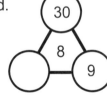 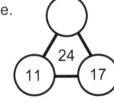

3. Examples:

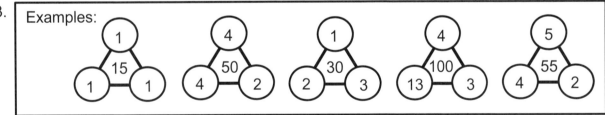

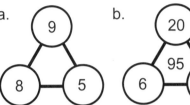 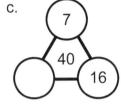 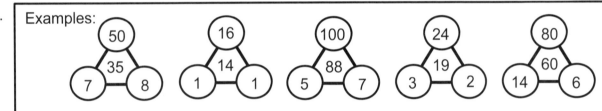

40. Function Finder 8

Each question shows a table for a different function machine. State the rule for the function machine and fill in the missing numbers.

1.

in	out
0	1
2	7
5	16
10	31
13	40
20	61
25	76
32	
	121

RULE:

2.

in	out
4	1.7
6.5	4.2
9.8	7.5
15	12.7
19.6	17.3
23.4	21.1
27.5	25.2
37.2	
	47.9

RULE:

3.

in	out
0	100
1	102
3	106
4	108
7	114
11	122
18	136
32	
	194

RULE:

4.

in	out
6	2
15	5
21	7
36	12
48	16
66	22
90	30
135	
	80

RULE:

5.

in	out
2	3
6	9
14	21
22	33
30	45
42	63
50	75
80	
	156

RULE:

6.

in	out
1	1
9	3
25	5
49	7
64	8
100	10
121	11
225	
	20

RULE:

Hints

1. Pattern Predictor 1 (p. 1)
- *Hint for question 1*: Stage 3 has 3 x 3 = 9 unshaded circles; stage 4 has 4 x 4 = 16 unshaded circles. So stage 9 has 9 x 9 unshaded circles.
- *Hint for question 5*: You can use guess-and-check to find which stage number has 400 unshaded circles. Stage 10 has 10 x 10 = 100 unshaded circles, which is too small; stage 30 has 30 x 30 = 900 unshaded circles, which is too large. Keep trying.
- *Hint for question 7*: Stage 3 has 2 rows of 3 shaded diamonds; stage 4 has 3 rows of 4 shaded diamonds. So stage 7 has 6 rows of 7 shaded diamonds.

2. Equality Explorer 1 (p. 3)
- *Hint for question 1*: The second balance implies that 2 squares are worth 18, so 1 square is worth 9. The third balance implies that 2 squares + triangle = 25. Since 2 squares are worth 18, the third balance implies that 18 + triangle = 25. So the triangle is worth 7.
- *Hint for question 2*: The third balance implies that 3 hearts are worth 36, so 1 heart is worth 12.
- *Hint for question 3*: Remove a diamond from each side of the second balance, and you are left with a circle balanced with 17. So the circle is worth 17.

3. Sequence Sleuth 1 (p. 4)
- *Hint for all questions*: Every odd stage number has shading outside the triangle. Every even stage number has shading inside the triangle. Every third stage number has a specific circle shaded. For example, the lower left circle is shaded for stages 1, 4, 7, 10, 13, 16, and so on. The overall shading pattern repeats every 6 stage numbers. For example, the lower left circle and the outside of the triangle are shaded for stages 1, 7, 13, 19, and so on.

4. Number Ninja 1 (p. 5)
- *Hint for question 1*: On the left side of the square, the sum of the top and middle numbers is $\frac{1}{8}+\frac{1}{2}=\frac{1}{8}+\frac{4}{8}=\frac{5}{8}$. Subtracting $\frac{5}{8}$ from 1 gives you the fraction in the bottom left circle. In a similar manner you can find all remaining circles.
- *Hint for question 2*: Recall the order of operations for +, −, x, ÷. First perform multiplication and division, in order of appearance from left to right. Then perform addition and subtraction, in order of appearance from left to right.

5. Function Finder 1 (p. 6)
- *Hint for question 2*: If 7 times the input equals 140, then the input is 140 ÷ 7.
- *Hint for question 3*: The rule for each table is described by a single operation, like "add 8", or "multiply by 3", or "subtract 5", or "divide by 7". Test out different rules on each row to see what works for all rows in a given table. In question 3a, the rule "add 9" works for the first row, since 3 + 9 = 12, but it does not work for the second row, since 5 + 9 ≠ 20. The rule "multiply by 4" works for the first row, since 3 x 4 = 12: does this rule work for all the other rows?

6. **Pattern Predictor 2** (p. 7)

- *Hint for questions 2 and 3*: Stage 4 has a group of 4 x 4 = 16 triangles on the left, another group of 4 x 4 = 16 triangles on the right, and a row of 4 triangles in the middle. In a similar manner, stage 6 has a group of 6 x 6 triangles on the left, another group of 6 x 6 triangles on the right, and a row of 6 triangles in the middle.
- *Hint for question 5*: You can use guess-and-check to find which stage number has 136 triangles. Stage 7 has a group of 7 x 7 triangles on the left, another group of 7 x 7 triangles on the right, and a row of 7 triangles in the middle. So stage 7 has 49 + 49 + 7 = 105 triangles, which is too few. Try a larger stage number and see what you get.
- *Hint for questions 8-13*: Each stage has a square of hearts, plus an additional 4 hearts on the corners. The side of the square has one more heart than the stage number. Stage 3 has a 4 x 4 square of hearts, plus an additional 4 hearts on the corners. Stage 4 has a 5 x 5 square of hearts, plus an additional 4 hearts on the corners. In a similar manner, stage 8 has a 9 x 9 square of hearts, plus an additional 4 hearts on the corners.

7. **Equality Explorer 2** (p. 9)

- *Hint for question 1*: The square on the left balances with the square on the right. Removing the squares leaves you with two clouds balanced with 18.
- *Hint for question 3*: The second balance implies that star + star + circle = 25. Since the first balance implies that star + circle = 19, the second balance implies that star + 19 = 25.

8. **Sequence Sleuth 2** (p. 10)

- *Hint for all questions*: The pattern repeats every 3 stages. The stage 1 shape repeats at stages 4, 7, 10, 13, 16, 19, and so on. The stage 2 shape repeats at stages 5, 8, 11, 14, 17, 20, and so on. The stage 3 shape repeats at stages 6, 9, 12, 15, 18, 21, and so on.

9. **Number Ninja 2** (p. 11)

- *Hint for all questions*: These number puzzles are perhaps best done with guess-and-check and a playful spirit. However, more formal reasoning can be used. For example, in question 4 the bottom right circle is 6 larger than the bottom left circle, since the sum of the bottom right and top circles (15) is 6 larger than the sum of the bottom left and top circles (9). Since the sum of the bottom left and bottom right circle is 10, this means the bottom left circle is 2 and the bottom right circle is 8: 2 + 8 = 10, and 8 is 6 more than 2.
- *Hint for question 6*: A possible number is 0.
- *Hint for question 12*: Rewrite each fraction shown using the common denominator of 6. Then focus on the numerators.

10. **Function Finder 2** (p. 12)

- *Hint for question 3*: The rule for each table is described by multiplication followed by addition, like "multiply by 4 and then add 9", or "multiply by 7 and then add 3." Test out different rules on each row to see what works for all rows in a given table. In question 3b, "multiply by 3 and then add 6" works for the second row, since 3 x 2 + 6 = 12, but it does not work for the third row, since 3 x 3 + 6 ≠ 17. The rule "multiply by 5 and then add 2" works for the second row, since 5 x 2 + 2 = 12: does this rule work for all the other rows? Also, note that when you input 0 in the first row, the multiplication part of the rule gives zero: so the output must equal the result of the addition part of the rule.

11. Pattern Predictor 3 (p. 13)
- *Hint for questions 1-6*: The number of stars starts at 6 and then increases by 4 each time.

stage	1	2	3	4	5	6	7	8	9	10
# stars	6	10	14	18	22	26	30	34	38	42

- *Hint for questions 7-12*: The number of unshaded circles starts at 3 and increases by 3 each time. The number of shaded circles starts at 4 and increases by 1 each time. The total number of circles starts at 7 and increases by 4 each time.

stage	1	2	3	4	5	6	7	8	9	10
# unshaded circles	3	6	9	12	15	18	21	24	27	30
# shaded circles	4	5	6	7	8	9	10	11	12	13
total # circles	7	11	15	19	23	27	31	35	39	43

12. Equality Explorer 3 (p. 15)
- *Hint for question 1*: The second balance implies that heart + triangle + heart + heart = 34. Since the first balance implies that heart + triangle = 20, the second balance implies that 20 + 2 hearts = 34, or that 2 hearts = 14.
- *Hint for question 2*: 3 stars + 3 squares = 36. Dividing both sides of the balance by 3 gives star + square = 12.

13. Sequence Sleuth 3 (p. 16)
- *Hint for all questions*: Every stage the time increases by 1 hour, 15 minutes. For every 4 stages the time increases by 5 hours.

14. Number Ninja 3 (p. 17)
- *Hint for questions 1b, 2b, and 3b*: To work backwards from end to start, always undo an operation with the opposite operation. In 1b, you end up with 14 and need to work backwards to find the start. Since adding 8 to a number results in 14, that number must be 14 − 8 = 6. Continuing to work backwards from 6, since tripling a number results in 6, that number must be 6 ÷ 3 = 2. So the starting number is 2, which can be confirmed by moving forward to the end: tripling 2 gives 6, and then adding 8 to 6 gives 14.

15. Function Finder 3 (p. 18)
- *Hint for question 1*: When you multiply 6 times 7 and then add 1 you get 43.
- *Hint for question 2*: When you find the average of 10 and 20 you get 15. In other words, when you add 10 and 20 and then divide the result by 2 you get 15.
- *Hint for question 3*: When you add 3 and 2 and then double the result you get 10.

16. Pattern Predictor 4 (p. 19)
- *Hint for all questions*: Stage 3 has 3 rows of 4 circles each, stage 4 has 4 rows of 5 circles each, stage 5 has 5 rows of 6 circles each, and so on. For example, stage 10 has 10 rows of 11 circles each. For each stage, half of the circles are shaded and half are unshaded.
- *Hint for question 8*: 45 shaded circles means there are also 45 unshaded circles, or 90 circles in total. You can use guess-and-check to determine the stage number that has 90 circles. For example, stage 10 has 10 x 11 = 110 circles, which is too large. Can you find a smaller stage number that works?

17. Equality Explorer 4 (p. 21)

- *Hint for all questions*: For each question the information from one balance can be used in another balance to determine a shape's value. In question 1, the first balance implies that parallelogram + pentagon + circle = 15. Since the second balance in question 1 implies that pentagon + circle = 11, the first balance implies that parallelogram + 11 = 15. So the parallelogram is worth 4.

18. Sequence Sleuth 4 (p. 22)

- *Hint for all questions*: Using tracing paper, or dark writing on regular paper, can help you move from one term to the next. For example, if you draw the first term "1" on tracing paper and then turn the paper over (like flipping the page in a book), you will get the second term.

19. Number Ninja 4 (p. 23)

- *Hint for all questions*: The methods for solving these puzzles are similar to those in Number Ninja 1.
- *Hint for question 1*: The number $1\frac{1}{2}$ must be in the circle to the right of $\frac{1}{6}$. If it were in any other circle the resulting side would add up to more than 2.

20. Function Finder 4 (p. 24)

- *Hint for all questions*: The focus of the rules for these questions is division. All rules involve either simply division ("divide by 6") or division by a number followed by adding another number ("divide by 2 and then add 5"). In the first row for question 3a, dividing 24 by 8 gives 3: does dividing by 8 work for the remaining rows? In the first row for question 3b, dividing 20 by 2 and then adding 1 gives 11: does dividing by 2 and then adding 1 work for the remaining rows?

21. Pattern Predictor 5 (p. 25)

- *Hint for questions 1-5*: The total number of unit squares is the square of the stage number: 3 x 3 = 9 for stage 3, 4 x 4 = 16 for stage 4, 5 x 5 = 25 for stage 5, and so on. The number of unshaded unit squares is the square of one less than the stage number: 2 x 2 = 4 for stage 3, 3 x 3 = 9 for stage 4, 4 x 4 = 16 for stage 5, and so on. The number of shaded unit squares starts at 1 for stage 1 and increases by 2 each time: 3 for stage 2, 5 for stage 3, 7 for stage 4, and so on. A good check of your answers is to make sure for each stage that the number of unshaded squares plus the number of shaded squares equals the total number of squares.

22. Equality Explorer 5 (p. 27)

- *Hint for question 1*: Remove a square from each side of the third balance and you are left with the cloud equaling 25.
- *Hint for question 2*: Remove a diamond from each side of the first balance and you are left with 2 circles equaling 14, or 1 circle equaling 7.
- *Hint for question 3*: Remove a pentagon from each side of the third balance and you are left with 3 hearts equaling 24, or 1 heart equaling 8.

23. Sequence Sleuth 5 (p. 28)
- *Hint for all questions*: The direction of the arrow repeats every 4 stages. For example, the arrow points up at stages 1, 5, 9, 13, 17, and so on. The shaded circle pattern repeats every 3 stages. For example, exactly 1 circle is shaded at stages 1, 4, 7, 10, 13, 16, and so on. The overall pattern repeats every 12 stages. For example, the arrow is pointing up and exactly 1 circle is shaded at stages 1, 13, 25, 37, 49, and so on.

24. Number Ninja 5 (p. 29)
- *Hint for question 2*: Be willing to explore and search to find the right combinations of operations. Patience and persistence will be rewarded with success.

25. Function Finder 5 (p. 30)
- *Hint for question 1*: When you multiply 4 times 10 and then divide the result by 2 you get 20.
- *Hint for question 2*: When you add 40 and 20 and then subtract 1 you get 59.
- *Hint for question 3*: When you multiply 9 times 3 and then multiply the result by 10 you get 270.

26. Pattern Predictor 6 (p. 31)
- *Hint for question 1*: One table has 5 seats, and then you add 3 more seats with each additional table: 8 seats for 2 tables, 11 seats for 3 tables, 14 seats for 4 tables, and so on.
- *Hint for question 2*: Build off answers from question 1, in which you find 26 seats for 8 tables. You have to add 4 more tables to get 12 tables, which means you add 12 more seats (3 seats per additional table): 26 + 12 = 38 seats for 12 tables.
- *Hint for question 3*: Build off answer from question 2, in which you find 38 seats for 12 tables. You have to add 12 more seats to get 50 seats, which means adding 4 more tables for a total of 16 tables.

27. Equality Explorer 6 (p. 33)
- *Hint for question 3*: The first balance implies that heart + pentagon = 100. Since the second balance implies that a pentagon is worth 3 hearts, the first balance implies that heart + 3 hearts = 100, or 4 hearts = 100. So 1 heart = 25.
- *Hint for question 4*: The first balance implies that 2 squares + octagon = 19. Since the second balance implies that octagon = square + 4, the first balance implies that 2 squares + square + 4 = 19. This means 3 squares + 4 = 19, or 3 squares = 15, or 1 square = 5.

28. Sequence Sleuth 6 (p. 34)
- *Hint for question 1*: The pattern repeats every fifth term, and this repetition can be used to determine later terms. For example, P occurs for terms 5, 10, 15, 20, 25, 30, and so on. This means P also occurs for the 780th term. Question 1f asks for the 782nd term: if the 780th term is P, then the 781st term is L, and the 782nd term is M.
- *Hint for question 4*: The pattern repeats every sixth term, and this repetition can be used to determine later terms. For example, H occurs for terms 6, 12, 18, 24, 30, and so on. This means H also occurs for the 126th term. Question 4f asks for the 125th term: if the 126th term is H, then the 125th term is g.

29. Number Ninja 6 (p. 35)
- *Hint for all questions*: The methods for solving these puzzles are similar to those in Number Ninja 3.
- *Hint for question 3*: The opposite of squaring is taking a square root. The square of 9 is 81, and the square root of 81 is 9. The square of 4 is 16, and the square root of 16 is 4.

30. Function Finder 6 (p. 36)
   - *Hint for questions 1, 2, 4, 6*: The rules for these tables can be described by a single operation, like "add 15" or "divide by 3".
   - *Hint for question 3*: The rule for this table involves multiplication followed by addition, like "multiply by 4, then add 3".
   - *Hint for question 5*: The square of 3 is 9.

31. Pattern Predictor 7 (p. 37)
   - *Hint for all questions*: The number of unit cubes is the cube of the stage number: 1 x 1 x 1 = 1 for stage 1, 2 x 2 x 2 = 8 for stage 2, 3 x 3 x 3 = 27 for stage 3, 4 x 4 x 4 = 64 for stage 4, and so on. The surface of the cube has 6 faces, and the number of unit squares on each face is the square of the stage number. So the number of unit squares on the surface of the cube is 6 times the square of the stage number: 6 x 1 x 1 = 6 for stage 1, 6 x 2 x 2 = 24 for stage 2, 6 x 3 x 3 = 54 for stage 3, 6 x 4 x 4 = 96 for stage 4, and so on.

32. Equality Explorer 7 (p. 39)
   - *Hint for question 1*: The first balance implies that heart + pentagon + heart = 23. Since the third balance implies that heart + pentagon = 18, the first balance implies that 18 + heart = 23. So the heart is worth 5.
   - *Hint for question 3*: Remove a square from each side in the first balance and you are left with 2 clouds = 18. Remove a cloud from each side in the second balance and you are left with 2 hexagons = 28.

33. Sequence Sleuth 7 (p. 40)
   - *Hint for all questions*: Using tracing paper, or dark writing on regular paper, can help you move from one term to the next. For example, if you draw the first term "A" on tracing paper and then rotate the paper clockwise 90 degrees (a quarter turn) you will get the second term. Also note that there are 4 terms per letter, and you can use this to predict the terms. Term 4 is the last appearance of the first letter A, term 8 is the last appearance of the second letter B, term 12 is the last appearance of the third letter C, and so on.

34. Number Ninja 7 (p. 41)
   - *Hint for question 1*: 2 x 7 = 14, 2 + 7 = 9.
   - *Hint for question 2*: (40 + 38) ÷ 2 = 39, 40 − 38 = 2.
   - *Hint for question 3*: 2 x (8 + 5) = 26, 2 x (8 − 5) = 6.

35. Function Finder 7 (p. 42)
   - *Hint for question 1*: When you add 13 and 27 you get 40. Taking the reciprocal of 40 gives you 1/40.
   - *Hint for question 2*: When you subtract 34 from 87 you get 53. Multiplying 53 by 10 gives you 530.
   - *Hint for question 3*: When you multiply 2 times 10 and then add 3 you get 23.

36. Pattern Predictor 8 (p. 43)

- *Hint for questions 1-5*: Look for patterns in the increase of the number of unit triangles from one stage to the next. For example:

stage	1	2	3	4	5	6	7	8
# of shaded unit triangles	1	3	6	10	15			

+ 2   + 3   + 4   + 5   and so on…

- *Hint for question 6*: Stage 3 has 9 unit squares, four 2 x 2 squares, and one 3 x 3 square: 9 + 4 + 1 = 14 squares of any size.
- *Hint for question 7*: Stage 4 has 16 unit squares, nine 2 x 2 squares, four 3 x 3 squares, and one 4 x 4 square: 16 + 9 + 4 + 1 = 30 squares of any size. Finding a pattern in the sums (9 + 4 + 1 followed by 16 + 9 + 4 + 1) will help you with later questions.

37. Equality Explorer 8 (p. 45)

- *Hint for question 2*: Remove a heart and a triangle from each side of the first balance and you are left with a heart balanced with 7.
- *Hint for question 3*: The first balance implies that 3 clouds + 3 pentagons = 30, which means cloud + pentagon = 10. The second balance implies that cloud + pentagon + circle = 15. Since the first balance implies that cloud + pentagon = 10, the second balance implies that 10 + circle = 15. So the circle is worth 5.

38. Sequence Sleuth 8 (p. 46)

- *Hint for all questions*: Finding a pattern will help you determine later numbers in the sequence without a lot of counting. In question 1, the sequence starts at 8 and increases by 5 each time, so the first eight numbers are 8, 13, 18, 23, 28, 33, 38, 43. To reach the 20th number, you will have to add 5 twelve more times to the 8th number, 43. So the 20th number is 43 + 5 x 12 = 43 + 60 = 103.

39. Number Ninja 8 (p. 47)

- *Hint for question 1*: When you multiply 9 times 7 and then subtract 4 you get 59.
- *Hint for question 2*: When you add 7 and 8 and then subtract the result from 50 you get 35.
- *Hint for question 3*: When you add 1 and 1 and 1 and then multiply the result by 5 you get 15.

40. Function Finder 8 (p. 48)

- *Hint for questions 1, 3*: The rules for these tables involve multiplication followed by addition, like "multiply by 5 and then add 2".
- *Hint for questions 2, 4, and 5*: The rules for these tables can be described by a single operation, like "add 7", "divide by 5", or "multiply by 2.5".
- *Hint for question 6*: The square root of 25 is 5.

Solutions

1. Pattern Predictor 1 (p. 1)

1. 81 unshaded circles

Stage 1 has 1 x 1 = 1 unshaded circle.
Stage 2 has 2 x 2 = 4 unshaded circles.
Stage 3 has 3 x 3 = 9 unshaded circles.
Stage 4 has 4 x 4 = 16 unshaded circles.

Stage 9 has 9 x 9 = 81 unshaded circles.
The number of unshaded circles equals
the square of the stage number.

2. 24 shaded circles

Stage 1 has 2 x 1 = 2 shaded circles.
Stage 2 has 2 x 2 = 4 shaded circles.
Stage 3 has 2 x 3 = 6 shaded circles.
Stage 4 has 2 x 4 = 8 shaded circles.

Stage 12 has 2 x 12 = 24 shaded circles.
The number of shaded circles is double
the stage number.

3. 255 circles

Stage 15 has 15 x 15 = 225 unshaded circles and 2 x 15 = 30 shaded circles. So the
total number of circles is 225 + 30 = 255.

4. stage 7

From question 2, the number of shaded circles is double the stage number. So we need
to find the answer to the question: If twice a number equals 14, then what is the number?
The answer is 7 since when you double 7 you get 14.

5. stage 20

From question 1, the number of unshaded circles is the square of the stage number. So
we need to find the answer to the question: If the square of a number equals 400, then
what is the number? The answer is 20 since 20 x 20 = 400. Note that 20 is the square
root of 400.

6. 10 unshaded diamonds

Stage 1 has 1 unshaded diamond, stage 2 has 2 unshaded diamonds, stage 3 has 3
unshaded diamonds, stage 4 has 4 unshaded diamonds, and so on. The number of
unshaded diamonds equals the stage number. So stage 10 has 10 unshaded diamonds.

7. 42 shaded diamonds

Stage 2 has 2 x 1 = 2 shaded diamonds, stage 3 has 3 x 2 = 6 shaded diamonds, stage 4
has 4 x 3 = 12 shaded diamonds, and so on. So stage 7 has 7 x 6 = 42 shaded
diamonds.

8. 144 diamonds

Stage 1 has 1 x 1 = 1 diamond, stage 2 has 2 x 2 = 4 diamonds, stage 3 has 3 x 3 = 9 diamonds, stage 4 has 4 x 4 = 16 diamonds, and so on. The total number of diamonds is the square of the stage number. So stage 12 has 12 x 12 = 144 diamonds.

9. stage 45

From question 6, the number of unshaded diamonds equals the stage number. So the stage number equals 45.

10. stage 10

From question 8, the total number of diamonds is the square of the stage number. So we need to find the answer to the question: If the square of a number equals 100, then what is the number? The answer is 10 since 10 x 10 = 100. Note that 10 is the square root of 100.

2. Equality Explorer 1 (p. 3)

1. square = 9, triangle = 7, hexagon = 18

The second balance tells us that 2 squares are worth 18, so 1 square is worth 9. Replacing the squares with 9 in the third balance implies 9 + triangle + 9 = 25, or 18 + triangle = 25. So the triangle is worth 7. Replacing the square with 9 and the triangle with 7 in the first balance implies 9 + 7 + hexagon = 34, or 16 + hexagon = 34. So the hexagon is worth 18.

2. star = 6, heart = 12, parallelogram = 14

The third balance tells us that 3 hearts are worth 36, so 1 heart is worth 12. Replacing the heart with 12 in the first balance implies that 2 stars + 12 = 24, which means that 2 stars are worth 12, or 1 star is worth 6. Replacing the star with 6 in the second balance implies that 2 parallelograms + 6 = 34, which means that 2 parallelograms are worth 28, or 1 parallelogram is worth 14.

3. circle = 17, diamond = 3, trapezoid = 5

Removing a diamond from each side of the second balance leaves a circle balanced with 17. So a circle is worth 17. Replacing the circle with 17 in the first balance implies that 17 + 2 diamonds = 23, which means that 2 diamonds are worth 6, or 1 diamond is worth 3. Replacing the diamond with 3 in the third balance implies that 3 + 2 trapezoids = 13, which means that 2 trapezoids are worth 10, so 1 trapezoid is worth 5.

3. Sequence Sleuth 1 (p. 4)

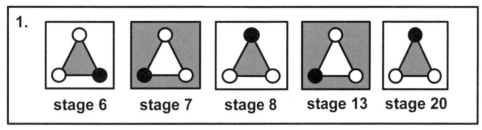

1.

stage 6   stage 7   stage 8   stage 13   stage 20

The shading pattern follows from two facts: (i) Outside the triangle is shaded for odd stage numbers, while inside the triangle is shaded for even stage numbers. (ii) Exactly one of the three circles is shaded for each stage number: lower left circle for stage 1, top circle for stage 2, lower right circle for stage 3, lower left circle for stage 4, top circle for stage 5, lower right circle for stage 6, and so on.

2. stage 26

The shading pattern repeats every 6 stage numbers. For example, the stage 1 pattern occurs again in stage 7, and the stage 2 pattern occurs again in stage 8. So the next stage number after stage 20 that has shading identical to stage 20 is stage 26.

3. stages 2, 4, 6, 8, 10, 12, 14, 16, 18, 20, 22, 24

The even stage numbers have shading inside the triangle.

4. stages 2, 5, 8, 11, 14, 17, 20, 23

The circle shading repeats every 3 stage numbers, starting with the top circle filled in at stage 2.

5. stages 2, 8, 14, 20

The stage numbers that have shading inside the triangle <u>and</u> the top circle filled in are the stage numbers that appear in the answers to question 3 <u>and</u> question 4, which are the numbers 2, 8, 14, 20. Note how this is consistent with the pattern repeating every 6 stage numbers.

6. stages 1, 7, 13, 19, 25, 31, 37, 43, 49

The shading repeats every 6 stage numbers, starting with 1.

4. Number Ninja 1 (p. 5)

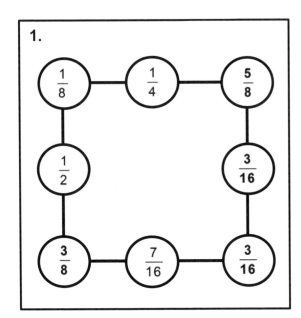

The sum of the left and middle numbers in the top side of the square is $\frac{1}{8} + \frac{1}{4} = \frac{1}{8} + \frac{2}{8} = \frac{3}{8}$.

The 3 numbers in the top side of the square add up to 1, so the number in the right circle at the top is $1 - \frac{3}{8} = \frac{5}{8}$.

The sum of the top and middle numbers in the left side of the square is $\frac{1}{8} + \frac{1}{2} = \frac{1}{8} + \frac{4}{8} = \frac{5}{8}$.

The 3 numbers in the left side of the square add up to 1, so the number in the left circle at the bottom is $1 - \frac{5}{8} = \frac{3}{8}$.

In a similar manner, one can fill in the remaining circles.

2.	1 + 4 x 5 = 21	or	1 + 5 x 4 = 21
	6 x 3 ÷ 2 = 9	or	3 x 6 ÷ 2 = 9

3.	6 x 9 – 5 = 49	or	9 x 6 – 5 = 49
	7 – 8 ÷ 4 = 5		

Recall the order of operations for +, –, x, ÷. First perform multiplication and division, in order of appearance from left to right. Then perform addition and subtraction, in order of appearance from left to right.

2. 1 + 4 x 5 = 21
     1 + 20 = 21
        21 = 21 ✔

    6 x 3 ÷ 2 = 9
      18 ÷ 2 = 9
          9 = 9 ✔

3. 6 x 9 – 5 = 49
     54 – 5 = 49
        49 = 49 ✔

    7 – 8 ÷ 4 = 5
       7 – 2 = 5
           5 = 5 ✔

5. Function Finder 1 (p. 6)

1. output is 84

12 x 7 = 84

2. input is 20

The input multiplied by 7 equals 140, so the input must be 140 ÷ 7 = 20.
To confirm: 20 x 7 = 140.

3a. Rule: multiply by 4	
in	**out**
3	12
5	20
8	32
12	48
15	60
21	84
25	100
40	**160**
52	208

3b. Rule: add 6	
in	**out**
1	7
4	10
6	12
9	15
14	20
18	24
25	31
38	**44**
57	63

3c. Rule: divide by 9	
in	**out**
27	3
45	5
72	8
90	10
99	11
135	15
180	20
225	**25**
333	37

3d. Rule: subtract 8	
in	**out**
10	2
14	6
18	10
20	12
25	17
50	42
74	66
88	**80**
100	92

6. Pattern Predictor 2 (p. 7)

1. 21 shaded triangles

A 3 x 3 square of triangles on the left, a 3 x 3 square of triangles on the right, plus a row of 3 triangles in the middle: 3 x 3 + 3 x 3 + 3 = 9 + 9 + 3 = 21.

2. 36 shaded triangles

A 4 x 4 square of triangles on the left, a 4 x 4 square of triangles on the right, plus a row of 4 triangles in the middle: 4 x 4 + 4 x 4 + 4 = 16 + 16 + 4 = 36.

3. 78 shaded triangles

A 6 x 6 square of triangles on the left, a 6 x 6 square of triangles on the right, plus a row of 6 triangles in the middle: 6 x 6 + 6 x 6 + 6 = 36 + 36 + 6 = 78.

4. 171 shaded triangles

A 9 x 9 square of triangles on the left, a 9 x 9 square of triangles on the right, plus a row of 9 triangles in the middle: 9 x 9 + 9 x 9 + 9 = 81 + 81 + 9 = 171.

5. stage 8

Stage 6 has 78 triangles and stage 9 has 171 triangles, so 136 triangles must in between stage 6 and stage 9. Using guess-and-check shows there are 136 triangles for stage 8: 8 x 8 + 8 x 8 + 8 = 64 + 64 + 8 = 136.

6. 465 shaded triangles

A 15 x 15 square of triangles on the left, a 15 x 15 square of triangles on the right, plus a row of 15 triangles in the middle: 15 x 15 + 15 x 15 + 15 = 225 + 225 + 15 = 465.

7. stage 12

Stage 9 has 171 triangles and stage 15 has 465 triangles, so 300 triangles must be in between stage 9 and stage 15. Using guess-and-check shows there are 300 triangles for stage 12: 12 x 12 + 12 x 12 + 12 = 144 + 144 + 12 = 300.

8. 40 hearts

A 6 x 6 square of hearts plus another 4 hearts on the corner: 36 + 4 = 40.

9. 85 hearts

A 9 x 9 square of hearts plus another 4 hearts on the corner: 81 + 4 = 85.

10. 148 hearts

A 12 x 12 square of hearts plus another 4 hearts on the corner: 144 + 4 = 148.

11. stage 9

Stage 9 has a 10 x 10 square of hearts plus another 4 hearts on the corner: 100 + 4 = 104.

12. 404 hearts

A 20 x 20 square of hearts plus another 4 hearts on the corner: 400 + 4 = 404.

13. stage 7

Stage 7 has an 8 x 8 square of hearts plus another 4 hearts on the corner: 64 + 4 = 68.

7. Equality Explorer 2 (p. 9)

1. cloud = 9

Removing a square from each side of the balance leaves 2 clouds balanced with 18, so 1 cloud is worth 9.

2. triangle + hexagon = 10

The balance tells us that 2 triangles + 2 hexagons = 20. Dividing both sides of the balance by 2 implies that triangle + hexagon = 10.

3. star = 6

The second balance implies that star + star + circle = 25. Since the first balance implies that star + circle = 19, the second balance implies that star + 19 = 25, which means that the star is worth 6.

8. Sequence Sleuth 2 (p. 10)

1.

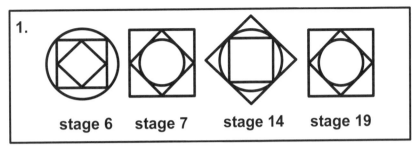

stage 6   stage 7   stage 14   stage 19

The shapes follow from the fact that the pattern repeats every 3 stages. The stage 1 shape also appears in stages 4, 7, 10, 13, 16, 19, and so on. The stage 2 shape also appears in stages 5, 8, 11, 14, 17, 20, and so on. The stage 3 shape also appears in stages 6, 9, 12, 15, 18, 21, and so on.

2. stages 2, 5, 8, 11, 14, 17, 20, 23

Since the stage 2 shape repeats every 3 stages.

3. stages 22, 25, 28

Since the stage 1 shape repeats every 3 stages: 1, 4, 7, 10, 13, 16, 19, 22, 25, 28.

4.

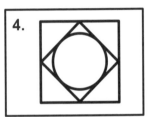

The stage 40 shape is the same as the stage 1 shape since the shape repeats every 3 stages: 1, 4, 7, 10, 13, 16, 19, 22, 25, 28, 31, 34, 37, 40.

5.

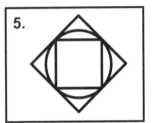

The stage 50 shape is the same as the stage 2 shape since the shape repeats every 3 stages: 2, 5, 8, 11, 14, 17, 20, 23, 26, 29, 32, 35, 38, 41, 44, 47, 50.

9. Number Ninja 2 (p. 11)

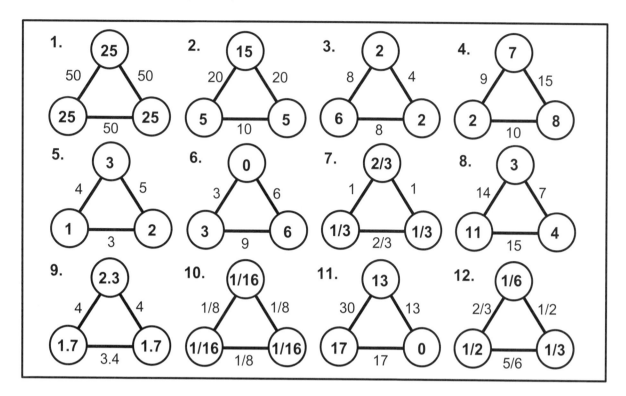

10. Function Finder 2 (p. 12)

1. output is 25

If you input 11, the output is

$2 \times 11 + 3 = 22 + 3 = 25$.

2. input is 5

Twice the input number plus 3 equals 13, which means twice the input number equals 10. So the input number is 5. To confirm: $2 \times 5 + 3 = 10 + 3 = 13$.

3a. Rule: multiply by 2 and then add 1

in	out
0	1
3	7
6	13
10	21
13	27
20	41
25	51
34	**69**
63	127

3b. Rule: multiply by 5 and then add 2

in	out
0	2
2	12
3	17
6	32
8	42
20	102
25	127
32	**162**
40	202

3c. Rule: multiply by 7 and then add 3

in	out
0	3
1	10
2	17
3	24
4	31
6	45
10	73
25	**178**
30	213

3d. Rule: multiply by 6 and then add 10

in	out
0	10
1	16
2	22
3	28
5	40
8	58
15	100
20	**130**
50	310

11. Pattern Predictor 3 (p. 13)

1. 22 stars

There are 6 stars at stage 1 and 4 more stars with each new stage. Stage 2 has 10 stars, stage 3 has 14 stars, stage 4 has 18 stars, and stage 5 has 22 stars.

2. 34 stars

There are 4 more stars with each new stage. Stage 5 has 22 stars, stage 6 has 26 stars, stage 7 has 30 stars, and stage 8 has 34 stars.

3. 62 stars

Stage 8 has 34 stars and it takes 7 more stages to get to stage 15. Since there are 4 more stars per stage, this adds 4 x 7 stars to 34. So the number of stars at stage 15 is 34 + 4 x 7 = 34 + 28 = 62.

4. stage 12

Stage 8 has 34 stars and it takes 16 more stars to get to 50 stars. Since there are 4 more stars per stage, it will take 4 more stages after stage 8 to get to 50 stars. So there will be 50 stars at stage 8 + 4, or stage 12.

5. 82 stars

Stage 15 has 62 stars, and it takes 5 more stages to get to stage 20. So at stage 20 there will be 62 + 4 x 5 = 62 + 20 = 82 stars.

6. stage 10

Stage 8 has 34 stars and it takes 8 more stars to get to 42 stars. It will take 2 more stages after stage 8 to get to 42 stars. So there will be 42 stars at stage 8 + 2, or stage 10.

7. 36 unshaded circles

The number of unshaded circles is 3 times the stage number: 3 x 1 = 3 unshaded circles at stage 1, 3 x 2 = 6 unshaded circles at stage 2, 3 x 3 = 9 unshaded circles at stage 3, and so on. So there are 3 x 12 = 36 unshaded circles at stage 12.

8. 20 shaded circles

The number of shaded circles is 3 more than the stage number: 3 + 1 = 4 shaded circles at stage 1, 3 + 2 = 5 shaded circles at stage 2, 3 + 3 = 6 shaded circles at stage 3, and so on. So there are 3 + 17 = 20 shaded circles at stage 17.

9. 43 circles

There are 7 circles at stage 1 and 4 more circles with each new stage number: 11 circles at stage 2, 15 circles at stage 3, 19 circles at stage 4, 23 circles at stage 5, 27 circles at stage 6, 31 circles at stage 7, 35 circles at stage 8, 39 circles at stage 9, and 43 circles at stage 10.

---

10. stage 8

From question 7, the number of unshaded circles is 3 times the stage number. So triple the stage number equals 24, which means the stage number is 8.

---

11. stage 22

From question 8, the number of shaded circles is 3 more than the stage number. So stage number + 3 = 25, which means the stage number is 22.

---

12. 83 circles

From question 9, stage 10 has 43 circles and there are 4 more circles with each new stage number. It takes 10 more stages to get to stage 20, so the number of circles at stage 20 is 43 + 4 x 10 = 43 + 40 = 83.

12. Equality Explorer 3 (p. 15)

1. heart = 7

The second balance implies that heart + triangle + heart + heart = 34. Since the first balance implies that heart + triangle = 20, the second balance implies that 20 + 2 hearts = 34. So 2 hearts = 14, or 1 heart is worth 7.

---

2. star + square = 12

The balance tells us that 3 stars + 3 squares = 36. Dividing both sides of the balance by 3 implies that star + square = 12.

---

3. parallelogram = 8

Removing a cloud from each side of the balance leaves 3 parallelograms balanced with 24, so 1 parallelogram is worth 8.

13. Sequence Sleuth 3 (p. 16)

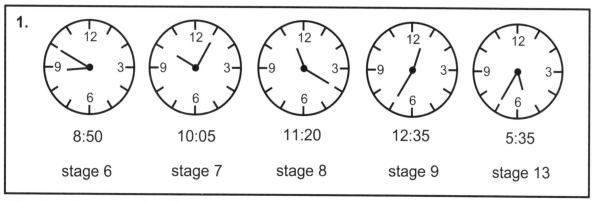

The time increases by 1 hour, 15 minutes from one stage to the next.

> **2. The stage 1 time is 2:35, the stage 5 time is 7:35, the stage 9 time is 12:35, and the stage 13 time is 5:35. The stage numbers increase by 4 and the times increase by 5 hours.**

A time increase of 1 hour, 15 minutes over 1 stage corresponds to a time increase of 5 hours over 4 stages.

> **3a. 10:35**

The stage 13 time is 5:35, so the stage 17 time is 5 hours later, or 10:35.

> **3b. 1:35**

The stage 17 time is 10:35 and time increases by 5 hours for every 4 stages. So the stage 21 time is 3:35, the stage 25 time is 8:35, and the stage 29 time is 1:35.

> **4. The stage 2 time is 3:50, the stage 6 time is 8:50, the stage 10 time is 1:50, and the stage 14 time is 6:50.**

The stage 2 time is 3:50 and time increases by 5 hours for every 4 stages.

> **5. 4:50**

The stage 14 time is 6:50 and time increases by 5 hours for every 4 stages. So the stage 18 time is 11:50 and the stage 22 time is 4:50.

14. Number Ninja 3 (p. 17)

> **1a. 56**

Tripling 16 gives 48. Adding 8 to 48 gives 56.

> **1b. 2**

Work backwards from end to start. If adding 8 to a number gives 14, then the number is 14 – 8 = 6. Continuing to work backwards, if tripling a number gives 6 then the number must be 6 ÷ 3 = 2. So the starting number is 2. Confirm this by moving from start to end: tripling 2 gives 6, and adding 8 to 6 gives 14.

2a. 33

Subtracting 11 from 77 gives 66. Dividing 66 by 2 gives 33.

2b. 21

Work backwards from end to start. If dividing a number by 2 gives 5, then the number is 5 x 2 = 10. Continuing to work backwards, if subtracting 11 from a number gives 10 then the number must be 10 + 11 = 21. So the starting number is 21. Confirm this by moving from start to end: subtracting 11 from 21 gives 10, and dividing 10 by 2 gives 5.

3a. 40

Dividing 70 by 5 gives 14. Adding 6 to 14 gives 20. Doubling 20 gives 40.

3b. 50

Work backwards from end to start. If doubling a number gives 32, then the number must be 16. Continuing to work backwards, if the adding 6 to a number gives 16 then the number must be 16 – 6 = 10. Going backwards one more time, if dividing by 5 gives 10 then the number must be 10 x 5 = 50. Confirm this by moving from start to end: dividing 50 by 5 gives 10. Adding 6 to 10 gives 16. Doubling 16 gives 32.

15. Function Finder 3 (p. 18)

1a. 46	**1b. 49**	**1c. 33**	**1d. 5**	**1e. 3**	**1f. 7**

The secret operation is to multiply the two numbers and then add 1.
For the examples given: 6 ♥ 7 = 6 x 7 + 1 = 42 + 1 = 43, 9 ♥ 10 = 9 x 10 + 1 = 91, 7 ♥ 4 = 7 x 4 + 1 = 28 + 1 = 29, 8 ♥ 3 = 8 x 3 + 1 = 24 + 1 = 25, 2 ♥ 5 = 2 x 5 + 1 = 10 + 1 = 11, and 3 ♥ 10 = 3 x 10 + 1 = 30 + 1 = 31.
For the questions: (a) 5 ♥ 9 = 5 x 9 + 1 = 45 + 1 = 46, (b) 16 ♥ 3 = 16 x 3 + 1 = 48 + 1 = 49, (c) 4 ♥ 8 = 4 x 8 + 1 = 32 + 1 = 33, (d) 5 ♥ 20 = 5 x 20 + 1 = 100 + 1 = 101, (e) 6 ♥ 3 = 6 x 3 + 1 = 18 + 1 = 19, (f) 7 ♥ 11 = 7 x 11 + 1 = 77 + 1 = 78.

2a. 10	**2b. 12**	**2c. 25**	**2d. 2**	**2e. 5**	**2f. 24**

The secret operation is to add the two numbers and then divide the sum by 2. In other words, the secret operation finds the average of the two numbers.
For the examples given: 10 ♦ 20 = (10 + 20) ÷ 2 = 30 ÷ 2 = 15, 13 ♦ 1 = (13 + 1) ÷ 2 = 14 ÷ 2 = 7, 25 ♦ 75 = (25 + 75) ÷ 2 = 100 ÷ 2 = 50, 14 ♦ 6 = (14 + 6) ÷ 2 = 20 ÷ 2 = 10, 12 ♦ 14 = (12 + 14) ÷ 2 = 26 ÷ 2 = 13, 5 ♦ 9 = (5 + 9) ÷ 2 = 14 ÷ 2 = 7.
For the questions: (a) 8 ♦ 12 = (8 + 12) ÷ 2 = 20 ÷ 2 = 10, (b) 3 ♦ 21 = (3 + 21) ÷ 2 = 24 ÷ 2 = 12, (c) 17 ♦ 33 = (17 + 33) ÷ 2 = 50 ÷ 2 = 25, (d) 2 ♦ 8 = (2 + 8) ÷ 2 = 10 ÷ 2 = 5, (e) 15 ♦ 5 = (15 + 5) ÷ 2 = 20 ÷ 2 = 10, (f) 24 ♦ 30 = (24 + 30) ÷ 2 = 54 ÷ 2 = 27.

3a. 20	3b. 28	3c. 32	3d. 2	3e. 7	3f. 3

The secret operation is to add the two numbers and then multiply the sum by 2.
For the examples given: 3 ♣ 2 = (3 + 2) x 2 = 5 x 2 = 10, 2 ♣ 7 = (2 + 7) x 2 = 9 x 2 = 18, 10 ♣ 1 = (10 + 1) x 2 = 11 x 2 = 22, 0 ♣ 8 = (0 + 8) x 2 = 8 x 2 = 16, 13 ♣ 2 = (13 + 2) x 2 = 15 x 2 = 30, 5 ♣ 4 = (5 + 4) x 2 = 9 x 2 = 18.
For the questions: (a) 3 ♣ 7 = (3 + 7) x 2 = 10 x 2 = 20, (b) 9 ♣ 5 = (9 + 5) x 2 = 14 x 2 = 28, (c) 10 ♣ 6 = (10 + 6) x 2 = 16 x 2 = 32, (d) 2 ♣ 4 = (2 + 4) x 2 = 6 x 2 = 12, (e) 8 ♣ 7 = (8 + 7) x 2 = 15 x 2 = 30, (f) 3 ♣ 10 = (3 + 10) x 2 = 13 x 2 = 26.

16. Pattern Predictor 4 (p. 19)

1. 30 circles

Stage 5 has 5 rows of 6 circles each, which means 5 x 6 = 30 circles.

2. 15 unshaded circles

Half of the 30 circles in stage 5 are unshaded.

3. 42 circles

Stage 6 has 6 rows of 7 circles each, which means 6 x 7 = 42 circles.

4. 21 shaded circles

Half of the 42 circles in stage 6 are shaded.

5. 110 circles

Stage 10 has 10 rows of 11 circles each, which means 10 x 11 = 110 circles.

6. 55 unshaded circles

Half of the 110 circles in stage 10 are unshaded.

7. stage 8, 36 unshaded circles

Stage 6 has 42 circles and stage 10 has 110 circles, so 72 circles must be in between stage 6 and stage 10. Using guess-and-check shows there are 72 circles for stage 8: 8 rows of 9 circles each, or 8 x 9 = 72 circles. Half of the circles are unshaded: 72 ÷ 2 = 36.

8. stage 9, 90 circles

Half of the circles are shaded, so 45 shaded circles implies 90 circles in total. Using guess-and-check shows there are 90 circles for stage 9: 9 rows of 10 circles each, or 9 x 10 = 90 circles.

9. 66 shaded circles

Stage 11 has 11 rows of 12 circles each, which means 11 x 12 = 132 circles. Half of these circles are shaded, or 132 ÷ 2 = 66.

10. 78 unshaded circles

Stage 12 has 12 rows of 13 circles each, which means 12 x 13 = 156 circles. Half of these circles are unshaded, or 156 ÷ 2 = 78.

11. 420 circles

Stage 20 has 20 rows of 21 circles each, which means 20 x 21 = 420 circles.

12. stage 7

Half of the circles are shaded, so 28 shaded circles implies 56 circles in total. Using guess-and-check shows there are 56 circles at stage 7: 7 rows of 8 circles each, or 7 x 8 = 56 circles.

17. Equality Explorer 4 (p. 21)

1. parallelogram = 4, pentagon = 8, circle = 3

The first balance tells us that parallelogram + pentagon + circle = 15. Since the second balance implies that pentagon + circle = 11, the first balance implies that parallelogram + 11 = 15. So the parallelogram is worth 4. The third balance tells us that parallelogram + circle = 7. Since the parallelogram is worth 4, the third balance implies that 4 + circle = 7. So the circle is worth 3. This means the second balance implies that pentagon + 3 = 11, so the pentagon is worth 8.

2. hexagon = 6, star = 7, triangle = 10

The second balance tells us that hexagon + star + triangle = 23. Since the first balance implies that hexagon + star = 13, the second balance implies that 13 + triangle = 23. So the triangle is worth 10. The third balance tells us that hexagon + star + star = 20. Again using that the first balance implies that hexagon + star = 13, the third balance implies that 13 + star = 20. So the star is worth 7. This means the first balance implies that hexagon + 7 = 13. So the hexagon is worth 6.

3. cloud = 11, heart = 2, square = 5

The third balance tells us that square + square + cloud = 21. Since the second balance implies that square + cloud = 16, the first balance implies that square + 16 = 21. So the square is worth 5. This means the second balance implies that 5 + cloud = 16. So the cloud is worth 11. Since the first balance tells us that cloud + heart + square = 18, this means 11 + heart + 5 = 18, or 16 + heart = 18. So the heart is worth 2.

18. Sequence Sleuth 4 (p. 22)

1.

| term 13 | term 14 | term 15 | term 16 | term 17 | term 18 | term 19 | term 20 |

2a.	2b.	2c.	2d.	2e.	2f.	2g.	2h.	2i.
Ɛ	Ɛ	Ɛ	∂	7	ㄥ	8	8	9	∂

19. Number Ninja 4 (p. 23)

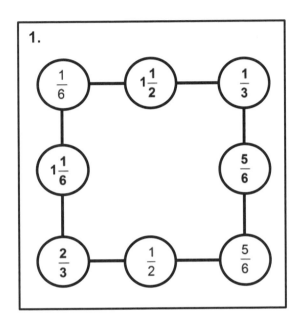

1.

The sum of the last 2 numbers in the bottom side of the square is $\frac{1}{2}+\frac{5}{6}=\frac{3}{6}+\frac{5}{6}=\frac{8}{6}$. The 3 numbers in the bottom side of the square add up to 2, so the number in the bottom left circle is $2-\frac{8}{6}=\frac{12}{6}-\frac{8}{6}=\frac{4}{6}=\frac{2}{3}$.

The sum of the bottom and top numbers in the left side of the square is $\frac{2}{3}+\frac{1}{6}=\frac{4}{6}+\frac{1}{6}=\frac{5}{6}$. The 3 numbers in the left side of the square add up to 2, so the number in the middle of the left side is $2-\frac{5}{6}=\frac{12}{6}-\frac{5}{6}=\frac{7}{6}=1\frac{1}{6}$.

In a similar manner, one can fill in the remaining circles. Note that $1\frac{1}{2}$ has to go in the middle of the top side, or else the right side will add up to more than 2.

2a. 2 + 3 x 6 = 20	2b. 12 − 2 x 3 = 6	2c. 20 + 3 − 10 = 13
2d. 4 x 8 − 3 x 9 = 5	2e. 6 x 6 ÷ 3 − 9 = 3	2f. 16 + 18 ÷ 6 + 11 = 30

Recall the order of operations for +, −, x, ÷. First perform multiplication and division, in order of appearance from left to right. Then perform addition and subtraction, in order of appearance from left to right.

a. 2 + 3 x 6 = 20
      2 + 18 = 20
          20 = 20 ✔

b. 12 − 2 x 3 = 6
        12 − 6 = 6
            6 = 6 ✔

c. 20 + 3 − 10 = 13
          23 − 10 = 13
              13 = 13 ✔

d. $4 \times 8 - 3 \times 9 = 5$
    $32 - 27 = 5$
    $5 = 5$ ✓

e. $6 \times 6 \div 3 - 9 = 3$
    $36 \div 3 - 9 = 3$
    $12 - 9 = 3$
    $3 = 3$ ✓

f. $16 + 18 \div 6 + 11 = 30$
    $16 + 3 + 11 = 30$
    $19 + 11 = 30$
    $30 = 30$ ✓

20. Function Finder 4 (p. 24)

1. output is 23

If you input 54, the output is

$54 \div 3 + 5 = 18 + 5 = 23$.

2. input is 18

The input divided by 3, with 5 then added to the result, equals 11. This means the input divided by 3 equals 6. So the input is $3 \times 6 = 18$. To confirm: $18 \div 3 + 5 = 6 + 5 = 11$.

3a. Rule: divide by 8

in	out
24	3
40	5
72	9
88	11
120	15
200	25
240	30
320	**40**
480	60

3b. Rule: divide by 2 and then add 1

in	out
20	11
40	21
100	51
200	101
500	251
800	401
900	451
1,000	**501**
2,400	1,201

3c. Rule: divide by 2 and then add 100

in	out
0	100
4	102
6	103
14	107
30	115
66	133
88	144
160	**180**
800	500

3d. Rule: divide by 12

in	out
24	2
36	3
60	5
72	6
120	10
180	15
240	20
360	**30**
540	45

21. Pattern Predictor 5 (p. 25)

1.

stage	1	2	3	4	5	6	7	8
# of unshaded unit squares	0	1	**4**	**9**	**16**	**25**	**36**	**49**
# of shaded unit squares	1	3	**5**	**7**	**9**	**11**	**13**	**15**
total # of unit squares	1	4	**9**	**16**	**25**	**36**	**49**	**64**

The total number of unit squares equals the square of the stage number (e.g., $8 \times 8 = 64$ for stage 8). The number of unshaded unit squares equals the square of one less than the stage number (e.g., $7 \times 7 = 49$ for stage 8). The number of shaded unit squares starts at 1 and increases by 2 for each new stage number (3 for stage 2, 5 for stage 3, 7 for stage 4, 9 for stage 5, and so on).

2. 100 unshaded unit squares

The number of unshaded unit squares equals the square of one less than the stage number: 10 x 10 = 100 for stage 11.

3. 27 shaded unit squares

The number of shaded unit squares equals 15 at stage 8 and increases by 2 with each stage number: 17 for stage 9, 19 for stage 10, and so on up to 27 for stage 14.

4. 225 unit squares

The total number of unit squares equals the square of the stage number: 15 x 15 = 225 for stage 15.

5. stage 18

The number of shaded unit squares equals 27 at stage 14, 29 at stage 15, 31 at stage 16, 33 at stage 17, and 35 at stage 18.

6.

stage	1	2	3	4	5	6	7	8
# of unshaded unit squares	1	4	9	16	25	36	49	64
# of shaded unit squares	8	12	16	20	24	28	32	36
total # of unit squares	9	16	25	36	49	64	81	100

The number of unshaded unit squares equals the square of the stage number (e.g., 8 x 8 = 64 for stage 8). The number of shaded unit squares starts at 8 and increases by 4 for each new stage number (12 for stage 2, 16 for stage 3, 20 for stage 4, and so on). The total number of unit squares equals the square of 2 more than the stage number (e.g., 10 x 10 = 100 for stage 8).

7. 144 unshaded unit squares

The number of unshaded unit squares is the square of the stage number: 12 x 12 = 144.

8. 48 shaded unit squares

The number of shaded unit squares equals 36 at stage 8 and increases by 4 with each stage number: 40 at stage 9, 44 at stage 10, 48 at stage 11.

9. 225 unit squares

The total number of unit squares is the square of 2 more than the stage number: 15 x 15 = 225 for stage 13.

10. stage 17

The number of shaded unit squares equals 48 at stage 11, and increases by 4 with each stage number: 52 at stage 12, 56 at stage 13, and so on up to 72 at stage 17.

22. Equality Explorer 5 (p. 27)

1. cloud = 25, triangle = 6, square = 11

Removing a square from each side of the third balance leaves a cloud balanced with 25. So a cloud is worth 25. Replacing the cloud with 25 in the first balance implies that 25 + triangle = 31, which means the triangle is worth 6. Replacing the triangle with 6 in the second balance implies that square + 6 = 17, which means the square is worth 11.

2. circle = 7, diamond = 5, hexagon = 2

Removing a diamond from each side of the first balance leaves 2 circles balanced with 14, which means 1 circle is worth 7. Replacing the circle with 7 in the third balance implies that diamond + 7 = 12, which means the diamond is worth 5. Replacing the diamond with 5 in the second balance implies that hexagon + 5 = 7, which means the hexagon is worth 2.

3. pentagon = 4, parallelogram = 13, heart = 8

Removing a pentagon from each side of the third balance leaves 3 hearts balanced with 24, which means 1 heart is worth 8. Replacing the heart with 8 in the first balance implies that 2 pentagons = 8, which means the pentagon is worth 4. Replacing the pentagon with 4 in the second balance implies 2 parallelograms + 4 = 30, or 2 parallelograms = 26, which means 1 parallelogram is worth 13.

23. Sequence Sleuth 5 (p. 28)

1.

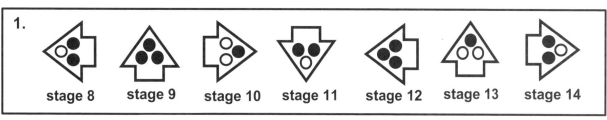

The direction of the arrow repeats every 4 stages. For example, the arrow points up at stages 1, 5, 9, 13, 17, and so on. The shaded circle pattern repeats every 3 stages. For example, exactly 1 circle is shaded at stages 1, 4, 7, 10, 13, 16, and so on. The overall pattern repeats every 12 stages. For example, the arrow is pointing up *and* exactly 1 circle is shaded at stages 1, 13, 25, 37, 49, and so on.

2.

Since the overall pattern repeats every 12 stages, stage 17 is the same as stage 5.

3.

Since the overall pattern repeats every 12 stages, stage 21 is the same as stage 9.

4.

Since the overall pattern repeats every 12 stages, stage 24 is the same as stage 12.

5. stage 14

Stage 2 + 12 = 14 is the same as stage 2.

6. stage 17

Stage 5 + 12 = 17 is the same as stage 5.

7. stages 1, 5, 9, 13, 17, 21, 25, 29, 33, 37, 41, 45, 49

Since the direction of the arrow repeats every 4 stages.

8. stages 1, 4, 7, 10, 13, 16, 19, 22, 25, 28, 31, 34, 37, 40, 43, 46, 49

Since the shaded circle pattern repeats every 3 stages.

9. stages 1, 13, 25, 37, 49

Since stage 1 has the arrow pointing up and exactly 1 shaded circle, and the pattern repeats every 12 stages.

10. stages 5, 17, 29, 41

Since stage 5 has the arrow pointing up and exactly 2 shaded circles, and the pattern repeats every 12 stages.

24. Number Ninja 5 (p. 29)

1.

$\dfrac{2}{15}$	$\dfrac{3}{10}$	$\dfrac{1}{15}$
$\dfrac{1}{10}$	$\dfrac{1}{6}$	$\dfrac{7}{30}$
$\dfrac{4}{15}$	$\dfrac{1}{30}$	$\dfrac{1}{5}$

The sum of the left number in the bottom row and the middle number in the middle row is $\dfrac{4}{15}+\dfrac{1}{6}=\dfrac{8}{30}+\dfrac{5}{30}=\dfrac{13}{30}$. The 3 numbers along either diagonal add up to 1/2, so the number in the top right square is $\dfrac{1}{2}-\dfrac{13}{30}=\dfrac{15}{30}-\dfrac{13}{30}=\dfrac{2}{30}=\dfrac{1}{15}$.
In a similar manner, one can fill in the remaining squares.

Examples:

2a.	**4 x 4 – 4 x 4 = 0**	4 x 4 – 4 x 4 = 16 – 16 = 0
2b.	**4 ÷ 4 + 4 ÷ 4 = 2**	4 ÷ 4 + 4 ÷ 4 = 1 + 1 = 2
2c.	**4 + 4 – 4 ÷ 4 = 7**	4 + 4 – 4 ÷ 4 = 4 + 4 – 1 = 8 – 1 = 7
2d.	**4 + 4 + 4 – 4 = 8**	4 + 4 + 4 – 4 = 12 – 4 = 8
2e.	**4 + 4 + 4 ÷ 4 = 9**	4 + 4 + 4 ÷ 4 = 4 + 4 + 1 = 8 + 1 = 9
2f.	**4 + 4 + 4 + 4 = 16**	4 + 4 + 4 + 4 = 16
2g.	**4 x 4 + 4 ÷ 4 = 17**	4 x 4 + 4 ÷ 4 = 16 + 1 = 17
2h.	**4 x 4 + 4 + 4 = 24**	4 x 4 + 4 + 4 = 16 + 4 + 4 = 24
2i.	**4 x 4 + 4 x 4 = 32**	4 x 4 + 4 x 4 = 16 + 16 = 32
2j.	**4 x 4 x 4 – 4 = 60**	4 x 4 x 4 – 4 = 64 – 4 = 60

25. Function Finder 5 (p. 30)

1a. 36	1b. 28	1c. 16	1d. 5	1e. 18	1f. 8

The secret operation is to multiply the two numbers and then divide the result by 2.
For the examples given: 4 ♠ 10 = 4 x 10 ÷ 2 = 40 ÷ 2 = 20, 8 ♠ 6 = 8 x 6 ÷ 2 = 48 ÷ 2 = 24, 3 ♠ 22 = 3 x 22 ÷ 2 = 66 ÷ 2 = 33, 6 ♠ 7 = 6 x 7 ÷ 2 = 42 ÷ 2 = 21, 3 ♠ 4 = 3 x 4 ÷ 2 = 12 ÷ 2 = 6, and 5 ♠ 10 = 5 x 10 ÷ 2 = 50 ÷ 2 = 25.
For the questions: (a) 8 ♠ 9 = 8 x 9 ÷ 2 = 72 ÷ 2 = 36, (b) 4 ♠ 14 = 4 x 14 ÷ 2 = 56 ÷ 2 = 28, (c) 16 ♠ 2 = 16 x 2 ÷ 2 = 32 ÷ 2 = 16 , (d) 5 ♠ 20 = 5 x 20 ÷ 2 = 100 ÷ 2 = 50, (e) 3 ♠ 18 = 3 x 18 ÷ 2 = 54 ÷ 2 = 27, (f) 8 ♠ 11 = 8 x 11 ÷ 2 = 88 ÷ 2 = 44.

2a. 25	2b. 46	2c. 17	2d. 6	2e. 19	2f. 35

The secret operation is to add the two numbers and then subtract 1.
For the examples given: 40 Ω 20 = 40 + 20 – 1 = 60 – 1 = 59, 25 Ω 10 = 25 + 10 – 1 = 35 – 1 = 34, 12 Ω 8 = 12 + 8 – 1 = 20 – 1 = 19, 14 Ω 14 = 14 + 14 – 1 = 28 – 1 = 27, 13 Ω 18 = 13 + 18 – 1 = 31 – 1 = 30, 9 Ω 4 = 9 + 4 – 1 = 13 – 1 = 12.
For the questions: (a) 11 Ω 15 = 11 + 15 – 1 = 26 – 1 = 25, (b) 17 Ω 30 = 17 + 30 – 1 = 47 – 1 = 46, (c) 6 Ω 12 = 6 + 12 – 1 = 18 – 1 = 17, (d) 6 Ω 13 = 6 + 13 – 1 = 19 – 1 = 18, (e) 7 Ω 19 = 7 + 19 – 1 = 26 – 1 = 25, (f) 35 Ω 95 = 35 + 95 – 1 = 130 – 1 = 129.

3a. 400	3b. 240	3c. 380	3d. 4	3e. 18	3f. 10

The secret operation is to multiply the two numbers and then multiply the result by 10.
For the examples given: 9 ↔ 3 = 9 x 3 x 10 = 27 x 10 = 270, 5 ↔ 9 = 5 x 9 x 10 = 45 x 10 = 450, 8 ↔ 1 = 8 x 1 x 10 = 8 x 10 = 80, 6 ↔ 6 = 6 x 6 x 10 = 36 x 10 = 360, 14 ↔ 5 = 14 x 5 x 10 = 70 x 10 = 700, 11 ↔ 4 = 11 x 4 x 10 = 44 x 10 = 440.
For the questions: (a) 8 ↔ 5 = 8 x 5 x 10 = 40 x 10 = 400, (b) 6 ↔ 4 = 6 x 4 x 10 = 24 x 10 = 240, (c) 2 ↔ 19 = 2 x 19 x 10 = 38 x 10 = 380, (d) 4 ↔ 7 = 4 x 7 x 10 = 28 x 10 = 280, (e) 3 ↔ 18 = 3 x 18 x 10 = 54 x 10 = 540, (f) 10 ↔ 10 = 10 x 10 x 10 = 100 x 10 = 1,000.

26. Pattern Predictor 6 (p. 31)

1.

# of tables	1	2	3	4	5	6	7	8
# of seats	5	8	11	14	17	20	23	26

There are 5 seats for 1 table and 3 seats added for each additional table.

2. 38 seats

There are 26 seats for 8 tables and 3 more seats for each additional table: 29 seats for 9 tables, 32 seats for 10 tables, 35 seats for 11 tables, and 38 seats for 12 tables.

3. 16 tables

There are 38 seats for 12 tables and 3 more seats for each additional table. Twelve more seats need to be added to have 50 seats, which means 4 more tables have to be added: 12 + 4 = 16 tables.

4. 92 seats

There are 50 seats for 16 tables and 3 more seats for each additional table. You have to add 14 tables to have 30 tables, which will add 3 x 14 more seats: 50 + 3 x 14 = 50 + 42 = 92 seats.

5. 23 tables

There are 50 seats for 16 tables and 3 more seats for each additional table. Twenty-one more seats need to be added to have 71 seats, which means 7 more tables have to be added: 16 + 7 = 23 tables.

6.

# of tables	1	2	3	4	5	6	7	8
# of seats	8	14	20	26	32	38	44	50

There are 8 seats for 1 table and 6 seats added for each additional table.

7. 80 seats

There are 50 seats for 8 tables and 6 more seats for each additional table: 56 seats for 9 tables, 62 seats for 10 tables, 68 seats for 11 tables, 74 seats for 12 tables, and 80 seats for 13 tables.

8. 10 tables

There are 50 seats for 8 tables and 6 more seats for each additional table. Twelve more seats need to be added to have 62 seats, which means 2 more tables have to be added: 8 + 2 = 10 tables.

9. 200 seats

There are 80 seats for 13 tables and
6 more seats for each additional table.
You have to add 20 tables to have
33 tables, which will add 6 x 20 more
seats: 80 + 6 x 20 = 80 + 120 = 200 seats.

10. 25 tables

There are 62 seats for 10 tables and
6 more seats for each additional table.
Ninety more seats need to be added
to have 152 seats, which means
90 ÷ 6 = 15 more tables have to be
added: 10 + 15 = 25 tables.

27. Equality Explorer 6 (p. 33)

1. hexagon = 8, cloud = 7

The first balance tells us that hexagon + cloud = 15. Since the second balance implies
that hexagon = cloud + 1, the first balance implies that cloud + 1 + cloud = 15. So 2
clouds + 1 = 15, or 2 clouds = 14, which means 1 cloud is worth 7. Replacing the cloud
with 7 in the first balance implies that hexagon + 7 = 15, which means the hexagon is
worth 8.

2. star = 11, circle = 22

The first balance tells us that star + circle = 33. Since the second balance implies that
1 circle = 2 stars, the first balance implies that star + 2 stars = 33. This means 3 stars
are worth 33, or that 1 star is worth 11. Replacing each star with 11 in the second
balance implies that circle = 2 x 11, or that a circle is worth 22.

3. heart = 25, pentagon = 75

The first balance tells us that heart + pentagon = 100. Since the second balance implies
that 1 pentagon = 3 hearts, the first balance implies that heart + 3 hearts = 100. This
means 4 hearts are worth 100, or that 1 heart is worth 25. Replacing each heart with 25
in the second balance implies that pentagon = 3 x 25, or that a pentagon is worth 75.

4. square = 5, octagon = 9

The first balance tells us that 2 squares + octagon = 19. Since the second balance
implies that an octagon = square + 4, the first balance implies that 2 squares + square +
4 = 19. This means 3 squares + 4 = 19, or that 3 squares = 15, or 1 square is worth 5.
Replacing the square with 5 in the second balance implies that octagon = 5 + 4, or that
an octagon is worth 9.

28. Sequence Sleuth 6 (p. 34)

1a. P	1b. N	1c. L	1d. M	1e. O	1f. M

The pattern repeats every 5 terms: L occurs for terms 1, 6, 11, 16, 21, 26, 31, 36, and so on, M occurs for terms 2, 7, 12, 17, 22, 27, 32, 37, and so on, N occurs for terms 3, 8, 13, 18, 23, 28, 33, 38, and so on, O occurs for terms 4, 9, 14, 19, 24, 29, 34, 39, and so on, P occurs for terms 5, 10, 15, 20, 25, 30, 35, 40, and so on.

2a. c	2b. b	2c. a	2d. b	2e. a	2f. c

The pattern repeats every 3 terms. In particular, the letter c occurs for terms that are multiples of 3: terms 3, 6, 9, 12, 15, 18, 21, 24, 27, 30, 33, and so on. (a) Term 18 is c, (b) term 33 is c, so term 32 is b, (c) term 66 is c, so term 67 is a, (d) term 93 is c, so term 92 is b, (e) term 99 is c, so term 100 is a, (f) term 300 is c.

3a. f	3b. g	3c. h	3d. i	3e. j	3f. k

Letter a occurs once, letter b occurs twice, letter c occurs 3 times, letter d occurs 4 times, letter e occurs 5 times, and so on. This implies a is term 1, the last b is term 1 + 2 = 3, the last c is term 3 + 3 = 6, the last d is term 6 + 4 = 10, the last e is term 10 + 5 = 15, the last f is term 15 + 6 = 21, the last g is term 21 + 7 = 28, the last h is term 28 + 8 = 36, the last i is term 36 + 9 = 45, the last j is term 45 + 10 = 55, the last k is term 55 + 11 = 66, and so on.

4a. H	4b. G	4c. H	4d. F	4e. f	4f. g

The pattern repeats every 6 terms. In particular, the capital letter H occurs for terms that are multiples of 6: terms 6, 12, 18, 24, 30, 36, 42, 48, 54, 60, 66, and so on. (a) Term 24 is H, (b) since term 24 is H, term 26 is G, (c) term 60 is H, (d) since term 60 is H, term 64 is F, (e) since term 120 is H, term 121 is f, (g) since term 126 is H, term 125 is g.

5a. C3	5b. C2	5c. A2	5d. C4	5e. C4	5f. B2

The pattern repeats every 12 terms: A1 occurs for terms 1, 13, 25, 37, and so on, B2 occurs for terms 2, 14, 26, 38, and so on. (a) Term 15 is the same as term 3, which is C3, (b) term 18 is the same as term 6, which is C2, (c) term 22 is the same as term 10, which is A2, (d) term 24 is the same as term 12, which is C4, (e) term 36 is the same as term 24 and term 12, which is C4, (f) term 38 is the same as term 26, term 14, and term 2, which is B2.

29. Number Ninja 6 (p. 35)

1a. 25

Doubling 19 gives 38. Subtracting 6 from 38 gives 32. Dividing 32 by 4 gives 8. Adding 17 to 8 gives 25.

1b. 53

Work backwards from end to start. If adding 17 to a number gives 42, then the number is 42 – 17 = 25. Continuing to work backwards, if dividing a number by 4 gives 25, then the number is 4 x 25 = 100. If subtracting 6 from a number gives 100, then the number is 100 + 6 = 106. If doubling the number gives 106, then the number is 106 ÷ 2 = 53. So the starting number is 53. Confirm this by moving from start to end: doubling 53 give 106, subtracting 6 from 106 gives 100, dividing 100 by 4 gives 25, adding 17 to 25 gives 42.

2a. 220

Dividing 64 by 8 gives 8. Adding 18 to 8 gives 26. Multiplying 26 times 9 gives 234. Subtracting 14 from 234 gives 220.

2b. 16

Work backwards from end to start. If subtracting 14 from a number gives 166, then the number is 166 + 14 = 180. Continuing to work backwards, if multiplying a number by 9 gives 180, then the number is 180 ÷ 9 = 20. If adding 18 to a number gives 20, then the number is 20 – 18 = 2. If dividing a number by 8 gives 2, then the number is 2 x 8 = 16. So the starting number is 16. Confirm this by moving from start to end: dividing 16 by 8 gives 2, adding 18 to 2 gives 20, multiplying 20 by 9 gives 180, and subtracting 14 from 180 gives 166.

3a. 15

Adding 3 to 6 gives 9. Squaring 9 gives 81. Subtracting 6 from 81 gives 75. Dividing 75 by 5 gives 15.

3b. 1

Work backwards from end to start. If dividing a number by 5 gives 2, then the number is 2 x 5 = 10. Continuing to work backwards, if subtracting 6 from a number gives 10, then the number is 10 + 6 = 16. If squaring a number gives 16, then the number is 4 (squaring -4 also gives 16, but we do not consider negative numbers in this problem). If adding 3 to a number gives 4, then the number is 4 – 3 = 1. So the starting number is 1. Confirm this by moving from start to end: adding 3 to 1 gives 4. Squaring 4 gives 16. Subtracting 6 from 16 gives 10. Dividing 10 by 5 gives 2.

30. Function Finder 6 (p. 36)

**1. Rule:
subtract 9**

in	out
15	6
22	13
30	21
39	30
47	38
51	42
76	67
167	**158**
202	193

**2. Rule:
multiply by 11**

in	out
0	0
2	22
3	33
5	55
8	88
10	110
12	132
15	**165**
25	275

**3. Rule:
multiply by 10
and then add 3**

in	out
0	3
1	13
4	43
6	63
9	93
12	123
20	203
27	**273**
41	413

**4. Rule:
divide by 6**

in	out
12	2
18	3
30	5
48	8
66	11
120	20
150	25
270	**45**
900	150

**5. Rule:
square the
input number**

in	out
3	9
4	16
5	25
7	49
8	64
10	100
12	144
15	**225**
20	400

**6. Rule:
add 15**

in	out
2	17
6	21
11	26
20	35
29	44
38	53
52	67
73	**88**
162	177

31. Pattern Predictor 7 (p. 37)

1. 27 unit cubes

Stage 3 has 3 layers of 3 x 3 unit cubes: 3 x 3 x 3 = 27 unit cubes.

2. 64 unit cubes

Stage 4 has 4 layers of 4 x 4 unit cubes: 4 x 4 x 4 = 64 unit cubes.

3. 54 unit squares

Stage 3 has 6 faces of 3 x 3 unit squares: 6 x 3 x 3 = 54 unit squares.

4. 96 unit squares

Stage 4 has 6 faces of 4 x 4 unit squares: 6 x 4 x 4 = 96 unit squares.

5.

stage	1	2	3	4	5	6	7
# of unit cubes	1	8	27	64	125	216	343
# of unit squares on the cube's surface	6	24	54	96	150	216	294

The number of unit cubes is the cube of the stage number. The surface of the cube has 6 faces, and the number of unit squares on each face is the square of the stage number. So the number of unit squares on the surface of the cube is 6 times the square of the stage number.

6. 1,000 unit cubes

Stage 10 has 10 x 10 x 10 = 1,000 unit cubes.

7. 600 unit squares

The stage 10 cube's surface contains 6 x 10 x 10 = 600 unit squares.

8. stage 8

From question 5, stage 7 has 343 unit cubes. Stage 8 has 8 x 8 x 8 = 512 unit cubes. So stage 8 is the smallest stage number for which there are at least 500 unit cubes.

9. 32 unit cubes

The shape has 2 layers of 4 x 4 = 16 unit cubes: 2 x 4 x 4 = 32.

10. 64 unit squares

The shape has 4 faces with 8 unit squares each and 2 faces with 16 unit squares each: 4 x 8 + 2 x 16 = 32 + 32 = 64.

32. Equality Explorer 7 (p. 39)

| 1. heart = 5, pentagon = 13, trapezoid = 28 |

The first balance tells us that heart + pentagon + heart = 23. Since the third balance implies that heart + pentagon = 18, the first balance implies that 18 + heart = 23. So the heart is worth 5. Replacing the heart with 5 in the third balance implies that 5 + pentagon = 18, which means the pentagon is worth 13. The second balance tell us that 2 hearts + trapezoid = 38. Since the heart is worth 5, the second balance implies that 10 + trapezoid = 38. So the trapezoid is worth 28.

| 2. parallelogram = 6, diamond = 3, circle = 10 |

The second balance tells us that 3 parallelograms = 18, which means 1 parallelogram is worth 6. The first balance implies that parallelogram + diamond + circle = 19. Since the parallelogram is worth 6, the first balance implies that 6 + diamond + circle = 19. So diamond + circle = 13. The third balance tells us that diamond + circle + circle = 23. Since we know diamond + circle = 13, the third balance implies that 13 + circle = 23. So the circle is worth 10. Replacing the circle with 10 in the third balance implies that diamond + 10 + 10 = 23, or diamond + 20 = 23. So the diamond is worth 3.

| 3. square = 12, cloud = 9, hexagon = 14 |

Removing a square from each side of the first balance leaves 2 clouds balanced with 18, which means 1 cloud is worth 9. Removing a cloud from each side of the second balance leaves 2 hexagons balanced with 28, which means 1 hexagon is worth is 14. Replacing the cloud with 9 and the hexagon with 14 in the third balance implies 9 + square + 14 = 35, or square + 23 = 35. This means the square is worth 12.

33. Sequence Sleuth 7 (p. 40)

1.

term 10   term 11   term 12   term 17   term 18   term 19   term 20   term 23

2a.   2b.   2c.   2d.   2e.   2f.

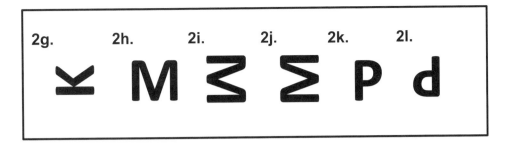

34. Number Ninja 7 (p. 41)

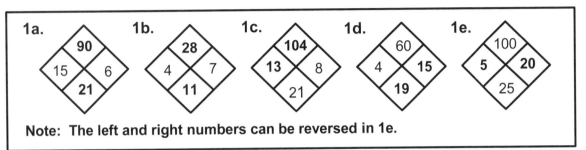

Note: The left and right numbers can be reversed in 1e.

The top number equals the left number times the right number (e.g., 90 = 15 x 6 in 1a).
The bottom number equals the left number plus the right number (e.g., 21 = 15 + 6 in 1a).

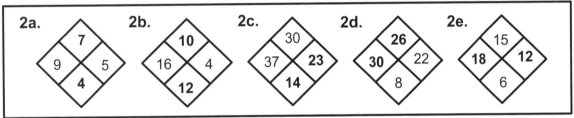

The top number is the result of adding the left number and right number, and then dividing the sum by 2 (e.g., 7 = (9 + 5) ÷ 2 in 2a). In other words, the top number is the average of the left and right numbers. The bottom number is the difference between the left number and the right number (e.g., 4 = 9 – 5 in 2a).

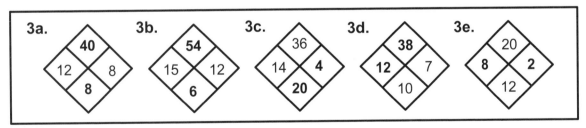

The top number is the result of adding the left number and right number, and then multiplying the sum by 2 (e.g., 40 = (12 + 8) x 2 in 3a). The bottom number is the result of subtracting the right number from the left number, and then multiplying the difference by 2 (e.g., 8 = (12 – 8) x 2 in 3a).

35. Function Finder 7 (p. 42)

1a. 1/12	1b. 1/53	1c. 1/60	1d. 28	1e. 73	1f. 24

The secret operation is to add the two numbers and then take the reciprocal of the sum.
For the examples given: 13 ☼ 27 = 1/(13 + 27) = 1/40, 75 ☼ 25 = 1/(75 + 25) = 1/100,
32 ☼ 43 = 1/(32+43) = 1/75, 17 ☼ 12 = 1/(17+12) = 1/29, 3 ☼ 5 = 1/(3+5) = 1/8,
11 ☼ 11 = 1/(11 + 11) = 1/22.
For the questions: (a) 4 ☼ 8 = 1/(4 + 8) = 1/12, (b) 9 ☼ 44 = 1/(9 + 44) = 1/53,
(c) 21 ☼ 39 = 1/(21 + 39) = 1/60, (d) 28 ☼ 9 = 1/(28 + 9) = 1/37,
(e) 15 ☼ 73 = 1/(15 + 73) = 1/88, (f) 24 ☼ 24 = 1/(24 + 24) = 1/48.

2a. 50	2b. 100	2c. 310	2d. 40	2e. 14	2f. 85

The secret operation is to subtract the second number from the first number and then
multiply the result by 10.
For the examples given: 87 ♪ 34 = (87 − 34) x 10 = 53 x 10 = 530, 20 ♪ 7 = (20 − 7) x 10 =
13 x 10 = 130, 100 ♪ 21 = (100 − 21) x 10 = 79 x 10 = 790, 15 ♪ 4 = (15 − 4) x 10 = 11 x
10 = 110, 54 ♪ 30 = (54 − 30) x 10 = 24 x 10 = 240, 22 ♪ 19 = (22 − 19) x 10 = 3 x 10 = 30.
For the questions: (a) 18 ♪ 13 = (18 − 13) x 10 = 5 x 10 = 50 (b) 28 ♪ 18 = (28 − 18) x
10 = 10 x 10 = 100, (c) 32 ♪ 1 = (32 − 1) x 10 = 31 x 10 = 310, (d) 40 ♪ 9 = (40 − 9) x 10
= 31 x 10 = 310, (e) 15 ♪ 14 = (15 − 14) x 10 = 1 x 10 = 10, (f) 85 ♪ 40 = (85 − 40) x 10 =
45 x 10 = 450.

3a. 42	3b. 45	3c. 17	3d. 11	3e. 13	3f. 35

The secret operation is to double the first number and then add the second number.
For the examples given: 10 ◄ 3 = 2 x 10 + 3 = 20 + 3 = 23, 50 ◄ 9 = 2 x 50 + 9 = 100 +
9 = 109, 15 ◄ 7 = 2 x 15 + 7 = 30 + 7 = 37, 75 ◄ 8 = 2 x 75 + 8 = 150 + 8 = 158,
100 ◄ 6 = 2 x 100 + 6 = 200 + 6 = 206, 5 ◄ 1 = 2 x 5 + 1 = 10 + 1 = 11.
For the questions: (a) 18 ◄ 6 = 2 x 18 + 6 = 36 + 6 = 42, (b) 20 ◄ 5 = 2 x 20 + 5 = 40 +
5 = 45, (c) 7 ◄ 3 = 2 x 7 + 3 = 14 + 3 = 17, (d) 11 ◄ 4 = 2 x 11 + 4 = 22 + 4 = 26,
(e) 44 ◄ 13 = 2 x 44 + 13 = 88 + 13 = 101, (f) 35 ◄ 10 = 2 x 35 + 10 = 70 + 10 = 80.

36. Pattern Predictor 8 (p. 43)

1.

stage	1	2	3	4	5	6	7	8
# of unshaded unit triangles	0	1	3	6	10	15	21	28
# of shaded unit triangles	1	3	6	10	15	21	28	36
total # of unit triangles	1	4	9	16	25	36	49	64

The total number of unit triangles is the square of the stage number.
The number of unshaded unit triangles is 0 at stage 1: 1 unshaded triangle is added to get stage 2 (0 + 1 = 1), 2 unshaded triangles are added to get stage 3 (1 + 2 = 3), 3 unshaded triangles are added to get stage 4 (3 + 3 = 6), 4 unshaded triangles are added to get stage 5 (6 + 4 = 10), 5 unshaded triangles are added to get stage 6 (10 + 5 = 15), 6 unshaded triangles are added to get stage 7 (15 + 6 = 21), 7 unshaded triangles are added to get stage 8 (21 + 7 = 28), and so on.
The number of shaded unit triangles is 1 at stage 1: 2 shaded triangles are added to get stage 2 (1 + 2 = 3), 3 shaded triangles are added to get stage 3 (3 + 3 = 6), 4 shaded triangles are added to get stage 4 (6 + 4 = 10), 5 shaded triangles are added to get stage 5 (10 + 5 = 15), 6 shaded triangles are added to get stage 6 (15 + 6 = 21), 7 shaded triangles are added to get stage 7 (21 + 7 = 28), 8 shaded triangles are added to get stage 8 (28 + 8 = 36), and so on.

2. 78 shaded unit triangles

The number of shaded unit triangles is 36 at stage 8: 9 shaded triangles are added to get stage 9, 10 shaded triangles are added to get stage 10, 11 shaded triangles are added to get stage 11, and 12 shaded triangles are added to get stage 12: 36 + 9 + 10 + 11 + 12 = 78.

3. 55 unshaded unit triangles

The number of unshaded unit triangles is 28 at stage 8: 8 unshaded triangles are added to get stage 9, 9 unshaded triangles are added to get stage 10, 10 unshaded triangles are added to get stage 11: 28 + 8 + 9 + 10 = 55.

4. 196 unit triangles

The total number of unit triangles is the square of 14: 14 x 14 = 196.

5. stage 30

The total number of unit triangles is the square of the stage number. The stage number is 30 since 30 x 30 = 900.

6. 14 squares

There are 9 unit squares, four 2 x 2 squares, and one 3 x 3 square: 9 + 4 + 1 = 14.

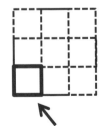
9 squares like these

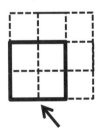
4 squares like these

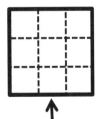
1 square like this

7. 30 squares

There are 16 unit squares, nine 2 x 2 squares, four 3 x 3 squares, and one 4 x 4 square:
16 + 9 + 4 + 1 = 30.

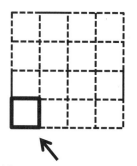 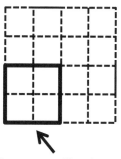 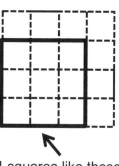 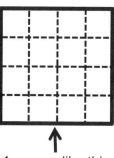

16 squares like these   9 squares like these   4 squares like these   1 square like this

8. 55 squares

There are 25 unit squares, sixteen 2 x 2 squares, nine 3 x 3 squares, four 4 x 4 squares, and one 5 x 5 square: 25 + 16 + 9 + 4 + 1 = 55.

9. 91 squares

There are 36 unit squares, twenty-five 2 x 2 squares, sixteen 3 x 3 squares, nine 4 x 4 squares, four 5 x 5 squares, and one 6 x 6 square: 36 + 25 + 16 + 9 + 4 + 1 = 91

10. 140 squares

49 + 36 + 25 + 16 + 9 + 4 + 1 = 140

11. 204 squares

64 + 49 + 36 + 25 + 16 + 9 + 4 + 1 = 204

37. Equality Explorer 8 (p. 45)

1. diamond = 9, star = 1, square = 15

The third balance tells us that 2 diamonds + 12 = 30, which means 2 diamonds = 18. So 1 diamond is worth 9. Replacing the diamond with 9 in the second balance implies that 3 stars + 6 = 9, which means 3 stars = 3. So the star is worth 1. Replacing each diamond with 9 and each star with 1 in the first balance implies that 9 + 9 + 1 + 1 + square + square = 50, which means 20 + square + square = 50, or 2 squares = 30. So 1 square is worth 15.

> **2. heart = 7, triangle = 3, parallelogram = 10**

Removing a heart and a triangle from each side of the first balance leaves a heart balanced with 7. So the heart is worth 7. Replacing the heart with 7 in the second balance implies that 7 + triangle + triangle = 13, or that 2 triangles = 6. So 1 triangle is worth 3. Replacing the heart with 7 and the triangle with 3 in the third balance implies that 7 + 3 = parallelogram. So the parallelogram is worth 10.

> **3. cloud = 8, pentagon = 2, circle = 5**

The first balance tells us that 3 clouds + 3 pentagons = 30, which means that cloud + pentagon = 10. The second balance implies that cloud + pentagon + circle = 15. Since the first balance implies that cloud + pentagon = 10, the second balance implies that 10 + circle = 15. So the circle is worth 5. Replacing each circle with 5 in the third balance implies that 2 pentagons + 5 + 5 = 14, or 2 pentagons + 10 = 14, which means 2 pentagons are worth 4. So 1 pentagon is worth 2. Replacing each pentagon with 2 in the first balance implies that 3 clouds + 2 + 2 + 2 = 30, or 3 clouds + 6 = 30, which means 3 clouds are worth 24. So 1 cloud is worth 8.

38. Sequence Sleuth 8 (p. 46)

> **1. next 3 numbers: 33, 38, 43   20th number: 103**

The sequence starts at 8 and increases by 5 with each new number. The first 20 terms are: 8, 13, 18, 23, 28, 33, 38, 43, 48, 53, 58, 63, 68, 73, 78, 83, 88, 93, 98, 103. Since the first number is 8 and there are 19 increases of 5 to reach the 20th number, the 20th number equals 8 + 5 x 19 = 8 + 95 = 103.

> **2. next 3 numbers: 19, 22, 25   25th number: 76**

The sequence starts at 4 and increases by 3 with each new number. The first 25 terms are: 4, 7, 10, 13, 16, 19, 22, 25, 28, 31, 34, 37, 40, 43, 46, 49, 52, 55, 58, 61, 64, 67, 70, 73, 76. Since the first number is 4 and there are 24 increases of 3 to reach the 25th number, the 25th number equals 4 + 3 x 24 = 4 + 72 = 76.

> **3. next 3 numbers: 825, 810, 795   15th number: 690**

The sequence starts at 900 and decreases by 15 with each new number. The first 15 terms are: 900, 885, 870, 855, 840, 825, 810, 795, 780, 765, 750, 735, 720, 705, 690. Since the first number is 900 and there are 14 decreases of 15 to reach the 15th number, the 15th number equals 900 – 15 x 14 = 900 – 210 = 690.

4. next 3 numbers: $4\frac{7}{8}$, $5\frac{1}{2}$, $6\frac{1}{8}$ **10th number:** $7\frac{3}{8}$

The sequence starts at $1\frac{3}{4}$ and increases by 5/8 with each new number. The first

10 numbers are: $1\frac{3}{4}$, $2\frac{3}{8}$, 3, $3\frac{5}{8}$, $4\frac{1}{4}$, $4\frac{7}{8}$, $5\frac{1}{2}$, $6\frac{1}{8}$, $6\frac{3}{4}$, $7\frac{3}{8}$.

5. next 3 numbers: $38\frac{1}{3}$, 36, $33\frac{2}{3}$ **10th number:** 29

The sequence starts at 50 and decreases by $2\frac{1}{3}$ with each new number. The first

10 numbers are: 50, $47\frac{2}{3}$, $45\frac{1}{3}$, 43, $40\frac{2}{3}$, $38\frac{1}{3}$, 36, $33\frac{2}{3}$, $31\frac{1}{3}$, 29.

6. next 3 numbers: 36, 45, 55   **15th number: 120**

The sequence starts at 1 and increases by 2 (to get to 3), then increases by 3 (to get to 6), then increases by 4 (to get to 10), then increases by 5 (to get to 15), then increases by 6 (to get to 21), and so on. The first 15 numbers are: 1, 3, 6, 10, 15, 21, 28, 36, 45, 55, 66, 78, 91, 105, 120.

7. next 3 numbers: $\frac{1}{16}$, $\frac{1}{32}$, $\frac{1}{64}$ **12th number:** $\frac{1}{512}$

The sequence starts at 4 and then each new number is half as large as the previous number. The first 12 numbers are: 4, 2, 1, $\frac{1}{2}$, $\frac{1}{4}$, $\frac{1}{8}$, $\frac{1}{16}$, $\frac{1}{32}$, $\frac{1}{64}$, $\frac{1}{128}$, $\frac{1}{256}$, $\frac{1}{512}$.

8. next 3 numbers: 72, 90, 110   **15th number: 240**

The sequence starts at 2 and increases by 4 (to get to 6), then increases by 6 (to get to 12), then increases by 8 (to get to 20), then increases by 10 (to get to 30), then increases by 12 (to get to 42), and so on. The first 15 numbers are: 2, 6, 12, 20, 30, 42, 56, 72, 90, 110, 132, 156, 182, 210, 240. Note how the numbers in this sequence are simply double the numbers in question 6.

39. Number Ninja 8 (p. 47)

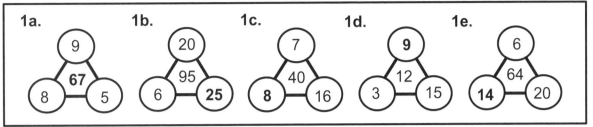

To calculate the middle number you multiply the lower left number with the top number and then subtract the lower right number: (a) 67 = 8 x 9 – 5, (b) 95 = 6 x 20 – 25, (c) 40 = 8 x 7 – 16, (d) 12 = 3 x 9 – 15, (e) 64 = 14 x 6 – 20.

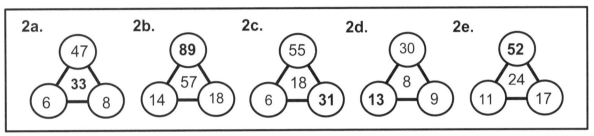

To calculate the middle number you add the two lower numbers and then subtract the result from the top number: (a) 33 = 47 – (6 + 8) = 47 – 14, (b) 57 = 89 – (14 + 18) = 89 – 32, (c) 18 = 55 – (6 + 31) = 55 – 37, (d) 8 = 30 – (13 + 9) = 30 – 22, (e) 24 = 52 – (11 + 17) = 52 – 28.

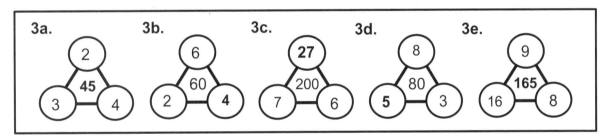

To calculate the middle number you add the 3 circled numbers and then multiply the result by 5: (a) 45 = (3 + 2 + 4) x 5 = 9 x 5, (b) 60 = (2 + 6 + 4) x 5 = 12 x 5 = 60, (c) 200 = (7 + 27 + 6) x 5 = 40 x 5, (d) 80 = (5 + 8 + 3) x 5 = 16 x 5 = 80, (e) 165 = (16 + 9 + 8) x 5 = 33 x 5.

40. Function Finder 8 (p. 48)

1. Rule:
multiply by 3
and then add 1

in	out
0	1
2	7
5	16
10	31
13	40
20	61
25	76
32	**97**
40	121

2. Rule:
subtract 2.3

in	out
4	1.7
6.5	4.2
9.8	7.5
15	12.7
19.6	17.3
23.4	21.1
27.5	25.2
37.2	**34.9**
50.2	47.9

3. Rule:
multiply by 2
and then add 100

in	out
0	100
1	102
3	106
4	108
7	114
11	122
18	136
32	**164**
47	194

4. Rule:
divide by 3

in	out
6	2
15	5
21	7
36	12
48	16
66	22
90	30
135	**45**
240	80

5. Rule:
multiply by 1.5

in	out
2	3
6	9
14	21
22	33
30	45
42	63
50	75
80	**120**
104	156

6. Rule:
take square
root of input

in	out
1	1
9	3
25	5
49	7
64	8
100	10
121	11
225	**15**
400	20

Math Analogies Level 3 Sample

Complete Each Math Analogy

33)

 :  :: 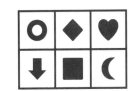 :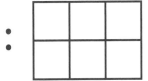

34)

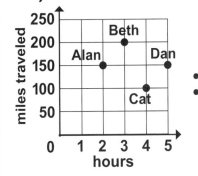 : Alan is fastest at 75 mph. Cat is slowest at 25 mph. :: 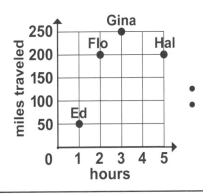 :

35)

1/2 of pizza

3/4 of pizza

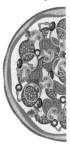 : $12 :: 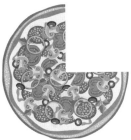 :

36)

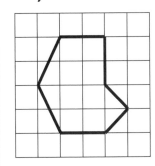 : area = 11 unit squares :: 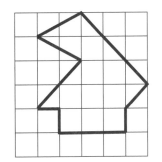 :